___LSAT Audio Study Guide! Ultimate Test Prep For The LSAT EXAM! Complete Review & Vocabulary Edition! By Dennis Reed

____

Introduction 7
A Brief History of the LSATS 8
Who Should take the Test? 8
Taking the LSATS 8
LSAT Dates 8
Cancelling the LSATS - What You Should Know 9
Digital LSATS 9
LSAT FAQ 11

What the LSAT exam entails? 11
Has the structure of the writing section changed 11
What can I expect if I choose to be waitlisted for my LSAT date and location? 11
Can I cancel my LSAT registration after the refund deadline has passed? 11

What represents a good score in the LSAT test? 11

Is the LSAT difficult to pass? 11

How much will I pay to participate in the LSAT? 11

I have a fee waiver. How do I withdraw my registration? 11

When will I receive my test score? 11

How do I cancel my score? 12

How long should I keep my records? 12

After failing the LSAT, how many times can retake? 12

What are the kinds of questions asked during the LSAT? 12

Scoring 160 on practice LSAT is it a good one? 12

For schools like Harvard, what's the LSAT score needed? 12

Is LSAT questions time sensitive? 12

If completing a digital LSAT, will test takers be able to use scratch paper? 12

How often will the digital LSATS be available throughout Canada and the United States? 12

Under what circumstances would I be ineligible to take the LSATS? 12

Is LSAT writing required in order to apply to law school? 13

When will my writing sample from my LSATS be available for my law school application? 13

What is the validity period of your LSAT score? 13

How long does it take for the LSAT results to be accessed? 13

Is it certain that law schools admit the candidates with the highest LSAT score? 13

What is a competitive LSAT score? 13

How to prepare adequately for the LSAT? 13

For a top school like Harvard, what is its average LSAT score? 13

What score is termed as a bad score on the LSAT? 14

Will the law schools I apply to actually read my writing sample? 14

What steps are the LSAC taking to protect my digital LSAT? 14

What are the things I need to come along with the LSAT? 14

Do you average LSAT scores? 14

Am I able to request accommodation for LSAT writing? 14

Will LSAT writing be available outside of North America? 14

Am I able to make adjustments to my biological information after I have registered for my LSATS? 14

Vital Information to Have Prior to Taking LSAT Test 15
How to Register for the LSAT 16
LSAT Scoring 16
Raw LSAT Score 17
LSAT Scaled Score 17
LSAT Percentile 18
LSAT Score / Percentile Conversion Chart 18

LSAT SCORES VS. GPA 20
WHY LSAT SCORES ARE SO IMPORTANT 20
LSAT Sections 21
When to Start Prepping for the LSATS 22
When to Take the LSAT 22
LSAT Study Strategies 25
Section Strategies 27
Analytical Reasoning 28
Steps to Take and Questions to Ask 30
What is an argument? 30
What is the Analysis of Argument? 30
The Stimulus 30
The Question Stem 30

LSAT Writing Sample Essay Guidelines and Tips 31
Attack the ArgumentAttack the Argument 31
Taking a Stance Quiz 1: Analysis of Argument 31
Creating Content 32

1) The Real-World Example: 32

2) The Theoretical Example: 32
Creating Content Analysis of Issue Examples 1 32

Creating Content Analysis of Examples 2 33

Creating a Strong Argument 33
Strengthening Arguments Example 1 34
Finding Errors 34
Circular Reasoning 34
Fallacy of the Insufficient Sample 35

The Fallacy of the Biased Sample 35
Straw Man 35
Ad hominem 35
Fallacy of Faulty Analogy 36
The "After This, Therefore, Because of This" Fallacy (Post hoc ergo propter hoc) 36
The "All Things are Equal" Fallacy 36
The Either-Or Thinking 37
Non Sequitur 37
Argument ad populum 37
Logical Reasoning 38
Logical Reasoning Tests Reasoning Ability 39
Logical Reasoning Tests Mental Discipline 40
Reading Comprehension 40
Timing 42
Basic Timing Instincts 43
Essential Timing Habits 45
The Challenges of Reading Comprehension 46
Timing Patterns for Top Scorers 47
Logical Reasoning: Sufficient Assumption & Supporting Principle 48
Conditional Logic 101 48
Conditional Logic Language 49
Conditional-Heavy Stimuli 49
Passage Topics 50
1. Science 50
2. Law 50
3. Cultural Studies 50
4. Society 51
Passage Structure 51
Presentation Styles 51

Case Study 51
Cause and Effect 51
Inquiry/Explanation 51
Writing Sample 52
How Should I Write My Essay? 53
Essay Section Template 55
Analytical Reasoning 56
Terms to Know 56
Logical Equivalence 57
Making Inferences 57
Revising Based on New Information 57
Comprehension 57
Tips and Tricks 58
Independence of Questions 58
Use Tools 58
Logical Reasoning 58
Terms to Know 59
Argument 59
Premise 59
Assumption 59
Conclusion 59
Specific Skills to Practice 60
Identifying Parts of an Argument and How They Relate to One Another 60
Identifying Similarities and Differences between Reasoning Patterns 60
Developing Well-Supported Conclusions 61
Using Analogy in Reasoning 62
Identifying Areas of Disagreement or Misunderstandings in an Argument 62
Explaining the Effect(s) of Additional Evidence on an Argument 63

Identifying Assumptions Used in Presenting an Argument 63
Finding and Using Principles and Rules in an Argument 64
Finding and Explaining Flaws in an Argument 64
Finding Explanations in an Argument 65
Reading Comprehension 65
Concepts to Understand 66
Main Idea or Primary Purpose 66
Explicitly Stated Information 66
Ideas that can be Inferred 66
Organization or Structure of a Passage 66
Specific Skills to Practice 67
Apply Information to New Context 67
Determine Word/Phrase Meaning from Context 67
Identify Principles Used in the Passage 68
Form Analogies for Arguments in the Passage 68
Identify the Author's Attitude from Tone and/or Language 69
Analyze the Effect of New Information on the Passage Disagreement 68
Compare Two Passages 68
Tips and Tricks 69
Identify Your Own Strategy 69
Mark Helpful Words and Points as You Read 69
Base Your Answer Only on Material Presented 69
Compare Two Passages Carefully 69

Some of the Most Challenging Passages Used in Previous Tests - Look Them Up and Use Them When Studying 69
How to Prepare for LSAT Reading Comprehension 71
Suggested Reading Material and the Proper Way to Approach the Material 71
Writing Sample 72
Writing Skills to Practice 73
Reasoning 73
Clarity 73
Organization 73
Language Usage 73
Mechanics 73
Legibility 74
One More Tip 74
Introduction to 10 Essential Grammar Rules for LSAT Writing 74
LSAT Vocabulary 79
Terms to Know 83
10 Fantastic LSAT Prep Tips 152
Stress and Time Management 153
Ladder of Difficulty 154
Diet tips for maintaining top mental health 154

Fats 154

Proteins 154

Carbohydrates 155

Vitamins and Minerals 155

Dinner the night before the test 156

Breakfast the morning of the test 156
Should You Take an LSAT Prep Course? 156
Top Ranked LSAT Prep Courses 157
ALPHA SCORE LSAT PREP 157
LSATMAX PREP COURSES 158
KAPLAN LSAT 158
MAGOOSH PREP LSAT 159
THE PRINCETON REVIEW LSAT 159
TESTMASTERS LSAT 159
BEST IN-PERSON LSAT PREP COURSE 160
POWERSCORE LSAT 160
7SAGE LSAT PREP 161
BEST LSAT PREP COURSES – 2019 COMPARISON 161
The Day of the Test 162
Law School Admissions Checklist 165
Conclusion 166

Introduction

The Law School Admission Test (LSAT) is conducted by the Law School Admission Council (LSAC) which is a nonprofit organization. Prospective students need to undergo an exam registration process by creating an account with the LSAC. This account will be used to register for the Credential Assembly Service (CAS). You are allowed to submit your entire law school credentials all at once to LSAC. After uploading all your application materials to the LSAC, it will be compiled in a report and forwarded to the law schools whenever you apply. Aside from administering the LSAT, the authentic and standardized LSAT PrepTests series will also be published by LSAC. You are required to seat for the

LSAT if you intend to apply for J.D. programs the U.S. or Canada law schools.

The LSAT is aimed at helping students develop their verbal reasoning and reading skills. The test measures the vital skills needed to excel in law school. Some of these skills include reading ability, ability to analyze complex words and make inferences from it, lastly the ability to examine and appraise the line of thought and argument of others.

There are three major sections in the LSAT consists of three types of multiple-choice sections The Reading Comprehension, Analytical Reasoning, and Logical Reasoning exams are multiple choice questions. Aside from this, candidates will also answer a writing section during the exam.
The total score for all the exam questions is 100, though the number of questions is not uniformly distributed among the sections.

Usually, $180 is charged to register for the LSAT, though this may vary based on individual case. For instance, late registration, making changes to the test date or location could cost an extra $90.

Another instance where you may need to spend more than the stipulated fee is if you live in a remote area from the closest test venue and you write to the LSAC, they will help set up a nonpublished test center at extra cost.
An additional cost of $275 or $370 will be charged for a domestic request, and international request respectively.

After your application to the law school, it's compulsory that you pay for the use of LSAC's

Credential Assembly Service (CAS) as it's a vital prerequisite in most law schools.

You need to pay $185 to sign up your CAS account and an extra fee of $30 for every law school that requests for your report. These reports are essential as law schools need it to check your academic record, LSAT scores, and other documents before offering you admission.

A Brief History of the LSATS

The LSAT was conceived out of a 1945 inquiry of a man named Frank Bowles, a Columbia Law School admissions director. About a more thorough admissions test that could be given for applicants. The primary goal of the experiment was to find a test that would correlate with year one grades as opposed to the bar passage rates. This led to an invitation of numerous representatives from some of the most prestigious law schools in the country, Harvard Law School and Yale Law School who ultimately accepted the invitation and began to develop and draft the first administration of the LSAT exam. New York University was also in correspondence by memorandum, and was openly unconvinced "about the effectiveness of an aptitude test as a method of selecting the most prepared and knowledgeable law school students." However, it was open to experimenting with the idea, as were other schools that were unconvinced. At a meeting in November 1947, with representatives of law schools extending beyond the original Columbia, Harvard, and Yale representatives, the design of the LSAT was determined. It was at this meeting that the issue of a way to test students who came from excessively "technical" backgrounds - causing them to be often considered deficient in the study of politics, literature, and history discussed but ultimately rejected. The first administration of the LSAT followed and took place in the year 1948.

Who Should take the Test?

Anyone intending to go to law school should take the LSAT. The score you receive is valid for three years following the date of the exam.

Taking the LSATS

The LSAT takes a total of 3 hours 45 min to complete while you will complete six sections of 35 minutes exam each. Note that there is a short 15 minutes break between the third and fourth sections for you to relax and probably take some snacks.

The breakdown of the LSAT exam is as follows: 4 scored, multiple choice, 1 unscored, trial multiple choice, writing sample (1 unscored), a break of 15 minutes after the third section.

A random ordered five multiple choice section will precede the break at the third section. Due to the random nature at which the multiple choice question is given, one won't be able to predict the unscored part correctly, so all section has to be treated with all seriousness. You won't be allowed to eat or take any drink except during the 15 minutes break, which means you will stay without food or drink for approximately 1 hour and 45 minutes. The only time you are allowed to take an excuse is when you need to use the restroom, and it's during a timed section. The LSAT test also teaches about endurance in addition to critical thinking.

LSAT Dates

The LSAT is held 4 times a year in: February, June, September/October, and December. The registration deadline for the test is about one month before the test date, but you should register several weeks earlier to get your first choice of date and location.
The tests are conducted on Saturdays (unless you observe Saturday Sabbath, then you can choose an alternate day of the week).

Check the LSAT test dates well in advance. You'll be surprised to see how quickly test locations fill up. Make sure to secure your seat in time!

Cancelling the LSATS - What You Should Know

Many students come out of the LSAT thinking that they did terrible, but this doesn't mean it's true. Cancelling the LSAT is irreversible. If you are considering a cancellation of a completed test, do not do it on the day of the test—you have six days to do so, and you should use that time to weigh your options carefully and rationally. Explain your situation to a trusted advisor for his or her opinion. If you had a lot of trouble with one section, remember that it could have been the experimental

section—you can determine which section was experimental by visiting LSAT discussion boards after the test. Also, remember that law schools are going to be notified that your score was cancelled at your request, which means you are going to have to explain yourself, although generally, a school won't penalize you for one cancellation, especially if your subsequent score is strong.
But re-taking the test may affect your application timing, which may affect your chances of admission. For example, if cancelling means you will be re-taking the LSAT in December, that will probably hurt your chances because your file won't be completed in time. Sometimes it's worth it, still, but this will be a factor for you to balance based on your own, unique situation.
Law schools will expect an explanation for repeated cancellations.

Digital LSATS

Beginning with the July 2019 LSAT, the LSAT will begin the long-awaited transition from the current paper-and-pencil LSAT to an electronic/digital form of the LSAT. Here are the Top 10 things to be aware of regarding the conversion:

1. The most significant thing about the upcoming digital LSAT, by far, is what is *not* changing: i.e., the substance and content of the exam. The LSAT's content will remain exactly the same as before, including the same number of sections, same section types, same question types, the same amount of time per section, etc.

2. The transition to the digital LSAT will begin with the July 2019 LSAT, so the upcoming March and June 2019 LSATs will be the same paper-and-pencil test as before.
3. The July LSAT will have 50% of the students taking the current paper-and-pencil exam, and 50% taking the new digital version – and no, you won't know until you get there which group you fall into! The good news? The July 2019 LSAT is the one time you can cancel your LSAT score *after* seeing your result.
4. Beginning with the September 2019 LSAT, the exam will be offered only in a digital format going forward.
5. The LSAC indicated that their studies show that test-takers were able to make the transition very easily. Going through the tutorial, I would agree: if you have even modest computer skills, it is very straightforward.
6. Since there is no difference at all in the content, there is no reason to change the nature of your preparation for the exam, other than to familiarize yourself with the digital LSAT. Symbolic logic, causation, logic games "trees" and all of the rest of standard-fare LSAT Prep remains just as applicable as before.
7. One procedural difference is that the LSAT's ungraded Writing Sample – historically the sixth and final section the LSAT – will now be offered separately from the rest of the LSAT. The good news is that you do not need to do the Writing Sample after your brain has been fried from doing five prior sections of the exam!

The scoring of the exam, and the speed in which you will get your score on the exam, also will not change.

8. You now *will* be given scratch paper, which can be used during the Analytical Reasoning section – that may turn out to be a nice benefit for some test-takers.
9. Candidly, the biggest impact the change to the digital LSAT is likely to have is on test-takers with extremely minimal computer skills. If you have even modest experience with computers, the transition is something to be aware of but not something to worry about. But you should go to the LSAC's online tutorial, spend a little time practicing with it, and see for yourself!

The Digital LSAT is the same multiple-choice exam as the paper-and-pencil LSAT, delivered on easy-to-use tablets instead of booklets. The tablets will be provided to test takers at the test center. The content will be the same and the structure of the test sections and the questions will be the same as the current LSAT. It is important to note that the test day will be shorter for test takers because the LSAT Writing will be (as of June 2019) administered separately from the LSAT multiple-choice test sections, online via a secure testing platform. Another important change for test takers will be that their answers will be selected on the screen by tapping on their answer choice. There will be no paper answer sheets. The tablet offers great features such as a timer with a five-minute warning, highlighting, and flagging to keep track of questions that a test taker may want to revisit in a section.

The transition to the Digital LSAT will begin in July 2019, when approximately half of the test takers will be assigned to take the test on a tablet provided by LSAC, and the rest will take the traditional paper-and-pencil test. After the July 2019 test, the LSAT will be digital in North America starting September 2019.

To help provide test takers with the tools and content to prepare effectively and confidently for the Digital LSAT, there have been many practice tests developed in order to assist applicants to get acquainted with the Digital LSAT practice site and format. We will continue to add practice tests in the weeks and months ahead. These practice tests provide an experience that mirrors the experience of the Digital LSAT. Prospective test takers can access the Get Acquainted site (including practice tests) on a laptop, desktop computer, tablet, or smartphone.

LSAT FAQ

What the LSAT exam entails?

The LSAT exam is divided into five sections with each of them containing a 35-minute multiple choice question.

Has the structure of the writing section changed?

No. LSAT Writing will use the same decision-prompt structure that candidates and schools are already familiar with from previous LSAT administrations. This structure is specifically designed to elicit the kind of argumentative writing that candidates will be expected to produce in law school. Candidates will still be given 35 minutes to write an essay in response to the prompt with which they are presented.

What can I expect if I choose to be waitlisted for my LSAT date and location?
We constantly monitor the seating capacity for upcoming LSAT administrations in the hope of assigning you to your preferred area when (and if) a test in that area becomes available. We will notify you by email about your test center assignment no later than one week before the test date.

Can I cancel my LSAT registration after the refund deadline has passed?
Yes. You may withdraw your LSAT registration in the LSAT Status section of your LSAC.org account once the refund deadline has passed and until 11:59 p.m. (ET) the night before the test. No refund will be issued, and your LSAT registration cannot be reinstated once withdrawn.

What represents a good score in the LSAT test?
For the five sections 35 minute multiple choice questions, one is expected to score 150 but scoring about 160 is a good score.

Is the LSAT difficult to pass?
It depends on your level of preparedness, but generally, most people confirm that it's difficult. This could be attributed to two main reasons, which are logic comprehension, which could be counter-intuitive and the mastery of the English language coupled with the limited time available.

How much will I pay to participate in the LSAT?
LSAT exam will cost you about $190, and you will

also receive a bonus score report.

I have a fee waiver. How do I withdraw my registration?
You may withdraw your LSAT registration in the LSAT Status section of your LSAC.org account once the refund deadline has passed. You must complete your withdrawal by 11:59 p.m. (ET) the night before the test. Once your registration is withdrawn, you may register for another LSAT that is administered within your two-year fee waiver period.

When will I receive my test score?
If you have an LSAC.org account, you will receive your score by email approximately three to four weeks after taking the test. Please keep your email address current in your LSAC.org account to receive your score promptly.

How do I cancel my score?
Beginning the day after the test, you may cancel your score on the LSAT Status page of your LSAC.org account. This option will only be available to you within six calendar days after the test. The deadline to cancel your score online will be 11:59 p.m. (ET) on the sixth day after your LSAT date.

How long should I keep my records?
Because some state bar associations inquire about the law school admission records of those seeking admission to the bar, you should maintain complete copies of all law school application records throughout the admission cycle and your law school career.

After failing the LSAT, how many times can retake?
You are permitted to take the LSAT thrice within two years.

What are the kinds of questions asked during the LSAT?
The LSAT comprises of various set of questions such as Multiple Choice, Essay Questions, Reading Comprehension, Logical & Analytical Reasoning

Scoring 160 on practice LSAT is it a good one?
Yes, 160 is a good score while practicing LSAT since the average is 150.

For schools like Harvard, what's the LSAT score needed?
To be considered for admission into Harvard Law School, you will need to score at least 170 in LSAT.

Is LSAT questions time sensitive?
Yes. Thirty-five minutes is earmarked for each section with 15 minute recess in-between the third and fourth sections.

If completing a digital LSAT, will test takers be able to use scratch paper?
Yes! LSAC will provide scratch paper and a pen for test takers to use during the test. Digital LSAT test takers will also be permitted to use their own pencil and eraser for making notes. We will provide a stylus that can be used to underline and highlight text on the tablet.

How often will the digital LSATS be available throughout Canada and the United States?

There will be nine LSAT administrations in the 2019–2020 testing year that begins in June 2019; only the June 2019 administration will be all paper-and-pencil. The July 2019 test will begin the transition to digital, and the September 2019 test will be all digital in the United States and Canada.

Under what circumstances would I be ineligible to take the LSATS?
If you served as a test center staff member for the LSAT, you may not take the LSAT in the subsequent 24-month period. If you plan to take the LSAT within 24 months of having either supervised an LSAT administration or worked as part of the testing staff at an LSAT administration, you must notify us when you register for the test. LSAC will review the request and either honor the registration or offer an alternative test center or date. We must receive your notification by the registration deadline of the requested test date. Failure to abide by this requirement may result in the initiation of a misconduct and irregularities proceeding.

Is LSAT writing required in order to apply to law school?
All candidates must have at least one writing sample on file—either from an earlier paper-and-pencil administration of the LSAT or from LSAT Writing—in order to have their Law School Report (which is a compilation of the candidate's undergraduate and graduate school records, admissions test score(s), writing sample(s), letters of recommendation, and other relevant materials) sent to any law schools to which they want to apply.

When will my writing sample from my LSATS be available for my law school application?
In many cases, LSAT Writing samples will be

processed within a week of completion. However, candidates are advised to allow three weeks for processing before their writing sample can be used to complete a Law School Report.

What is the validity period of your LSAT score?
The validity period of your LSAT is five years.

How long does it take for the LSAT results to be accessed?
Within three weeks, you should receive your test results.

Is it certain that law schools admit the candidates with the highest LSAT score?
Well, most law schools place significant emphasis on the candidates with the highest LSAT score.

What is a competitive LSAT score?
An LSAT score of 171 and above which is well more than the 150 average is termed a competitive score.

How to prepare adequately for the LSAT?
You are required to spend hours practicing and reviewing test questions and other instructional guides every week.

For a top school like Harvard, what is its average LSAT score?
Harvard Law School fixes 170 as its average LSAT score.

What score is termed as a bad score on the LSAT?
Any score below 145 is termed as a bad score.

Will the law schools I apply to actually read my writing sample?
Most schools use LSAT candidate writing samples as a part of the admission process. However, each school uses writing samples in its own way. LSAC expects that schools will rely more on the writing sample in the future since writing samples from LSAT Writing will be easier to read than the previously handwritten essays.

What steps are the LSAC taking to protect my digital LSAT?
Initial reviews of LSAT Writing videos will be conducted by trained proctors in a secure, supervised environment that does not allow any images to be copied from the videos being reviewed. If a video is flagged for suspicious behavior or test conduct violations, LSAC Test Security staff will review it through an encrypted portal that prevents any images from being copied for later use.

What are the things I need to come along with the LSAT?
You are required to come along with your admission tag and photo, a government-issued ID, writing materials (pencils and erasers), and any light snack.

Do you average LSAT scores?
Perhaps you have tried the LSAT more than once, your score will not be averaged, and instead, it will choose the one you scored highest.

Am I able to request accommodation for LSAT writing?
Yes. *Starting with the June 2019 test registration period*, candidates will submit requests for accommodations for LSAT Writing at the same time they request accommodations for the LSAT, using the same form. The process for reviewing accommodation requests will not change.

Will LSAT writing be available outside of North America?
Yes. LSAT Writing will be available in all locations with access to the Internet when it launches in June 2019.

Am I able to make adjustments to my biological information after I have registered for my LSATS?
Complete, sign, and send in the LSAC Biographical Information Changes form, with a copy of your ID if you need to correct your name, date of birth, or Social Security/Social Insurance number. You can make any other changes right in your LSAC.org account. Note: To be admitted to the test center, the first and last name listed on your ID must match exactly the first and last name printed on your LSAT Admission Ticket.

Vital Information to Have Prior to Taking LSAT Test

1. You Can Study For The LSAT

You will be misled by several people that your LSAT score measures some natural, unattainable, and static intelligent aspect of you. This is a misconception and a fallacy. Rather, the LSAT score measures the skills you or anyone else can acquire through study.

Studying for the LSAT is likened to taking a mathematics class. Some basic rules and methods will be learnt which you will need to apply to solve questions while improving on your knowledge with each lesson.

One thing you won't like to do is to miss a lesson as it will affect your learning process. Think about what transpired the last time you missed a math class session? Yeah, you felt lost all through the next math class.

Relating this to the LSAT prep which can be so boring if your instructor is not also making you get interested. That's why we ensure you study for your LSAT while having as much fun as you can. If you attend all your lessons, and take due diligence to do your homework, then your LSAT score will drastically improve.

2. Studying For The LSAT Will Make You Smarter

The LSAT is nothing like a traditional college exam. On the LSAT there will be no information dumping frenzy like writing long lists of facts or knowing vocabulary. Instead, the LSAT will test your ability to - to put it frankly - recognize "B.S."

The LSAT is a test of logic and how well you can apply it to certain situations and circumstances. While memorizing information and knowing a ton of terms and facts is great, logic is the one thing that you must constantly use on a daily basis (think back to that last cheesy "get rich quick" infomercial or ad you saw - hopefully your logic allowed you to realize that getting rich isn't going to be such a simple and easy process). So unlike your typical college exam, studying for the LSAT is actually going to help make you wiser, without filling your head with useless facts.

3. <u>The LSAT Is Extremely Hard</u>

The LSAT includes around 100 questions and is scored on a scale from 120 to 180. Typically, most people will end up scoring around 152 (meaning that most people miss around 45 questions). Given the numbers, if the LSAT actually gave letter grades like a typical exam, the reality is that most people would actually get an F. Can you imagine a professor that curves the class grades so that almost everyone would fail? Well, welcome to the LSAT.

While the above numbers and facts can be a little bit intimidating, don't stress yourself out too much. The reality is you can actually miss about 10 questions on your LSAT and still score higher than 99 percent of all other LSAT takers. While the exam is extremely tough, you don't have to be perfect to get an awesome LSAT score.

4. <u>You Can Retake The LSAT And Law Schools Will Only Count Your Highest LSAT</u>

This should help take some of the pressure off: these days most law schools are only interested in your highest LSAT score. Law schools only have to report their students' highest LSAT scores for their official stats, which also get churned into the U.S. News law school rankings (often referred to as "*the* rankings"). So even the schools that use a more "holistic" approach have an incentive to only care about your highest LSAT score.

June is early enough for you to have a complete meltdown during the LSAT, retake in September, and still apply to law school early in the cycle.

5. <u>Your Diagnostic LSAT Score Doesn't Mean Much</u>
I've been preparing students for the LSAT for about three years now. Before every diagnostic LSAT, I tell my students not to worry about their first practice LSAT score.
But people always freak out. "Maybe my mother was wrong. Maybe I'm not special." Sigh.
Taking a diagnostic LSAT before any LSAT prep will let you to track your progress, and this will make prepping more rewarding. Your first practice LSAT score is not a good predictor of your best LSAT score. I have personally seen many students improve on their first practice LSAT score by more than 20 points.
So try to relax.

How to Register for the LSAT

LSAC account registration is the first step to take, and it can be completed right here. Once this is done, you will be able to achieve the following:

- Register for the LSAT
- Buy materials to prepare for the test
- Register for law school forums
- Apply online to law schools

The LSAC registration takes you to the next step where you pick your test date and finalize your LSAT registration. It's part of the test preparation to know your test date beforehand, and it's also helpful to choose the most suitable date.

Next is for you to pay the stipulated fee through any of the following means: MasterCard, VISA, American Express, or DISCOVER. (here's a list of the charges).

LSAT Scoring

Your total score in the LSAT test is computed based on how well you performed in the four scored exam sections, namely:

- Reading Comprehension
- Analytical Reasoning
- Logical Reasoning (2 sections)

There is another section which is unscored as it's a trial section meant for research to determine the psychometric data on the consistency of the test. The Writing Sample also doesn't contribute to the final score as it's unscored.

There are about 100 questions distributed among the four scored sections, and each is allotted one point each. There is no bias with any section as the score is the same for all the sections.
You get a point for each correctly answered question, and no point is given for wrongly answered question; no negative point allocation or partial score.
So, it's imperative that you answer all questions as best as you can and attempt all questions if time permits.

The number of answered correctly answered multiple choice questions is your raw score. Once this score is known, it's easy to calculate the total score through a conversion table. The conversion table for each test is posted by LSAC and can be accessed on lsat.magoosh.com. Although each tests conversion table is slightly different, they have a relatively consistent number. LSAC uploads your raw score into a very complicated algorithm known as equating which factor in your test difficulty as against the previous tests and total questions. Below is an example of a conversion table created by finding the average of the 15 most recent LSAT conversion tables for a robust and reliable estimate.

Raw LSAT Score

The total amount of questions correctly answered is referred to as your Raw LSAT Score. Typically, the LSAT test will comprise of about 100 to 103 questions each, and your Raw LSAT Score could fall between any of the numbers from 0 to 100 or 103. For computing LSAT Raw Score, there will be no deduction of the mark if you get an answer wrong and all questions carry equal score. This implies that the difficult questions and easy ones carry the same score.

LSAT Tip: If you realize your time is almost up, you can move on to the simpler questions since they carry the same score as the harder ones. With this, you stand a better chance of having a higher Raw Score.

LSAT Scaled Score

Raw LSAT Scores are converted into the LSAT Scaled Scores, which ranges from 120 to 180. So if you scored 0 on the Raw LSAT Score (0 questions right) you would likely have an LSAT Scaled Score of 120 and if your Raw LSAT Score was 101 you would likely have an LSAT Scaled Score of 180. The conversion process is done by using a statistical procedure called equating. Equating adjusts for the differences in difficulty between different LSAT tests. For example, the October 1997 LSAT was harder than the June 2007 LSAT and so if you wrote both tests and your Raw LSAT Score on both was 55 your LSAT Scaled Score for the June 2007 LSAT would be 149 and for the October 1997 LSAT it would be 150. Generally the same Raw LSAT Score will produce the same or very similar LSAT Scaled Scores. The Scaled Scores below converted from the raw score are approximate, for your exact scaled score refer to the scoring page of the LSAT you are scoring.

LSAT Percentile

A percentile rank is also reported for each LSAT score, reflecting the percentage of candidates scoring below your reported test score. While the LSAT Scaled Score is based on the specific LSAT test that you wrote, the LSAT Percentile for a score is based on the distribution of scores for the three-year period prior to the year in which the score is reported. Your percentile rank tells you the percentage of scaled scores in the last three years that your score beats. For example if your LSAT Scaled Score is 157 you will have a percentile rank of approximately 75% meaning that your Scaled Score of 157 is better than 75% of the LSAT Scaled Scores for the last three years. The Percentile Scores below are the scores for the period from June, 2006 to February 2009. They include the statistical analysis of 429,816 LSAT scores over this 3 year period. Actual percentile rankings on your LSAT may vary slightly.

LSAT Score / Percentile Conversion Chart

For example, using the table below if you scored 65 questions right out of 101 questions on the LSAT your LSAT Raw Score is 65, your LSAT Scaled Score is 157, and your Percentile Rank is 70.9%ile. So while you got 65% of the questions right you are in the 70.9th percentile meaning your LSAT Scaled Score was better than 70.9% of the people who wrote the LSAT in the last three years. Note that the table below is a guide and minor variances will occur with each writing of the LSAT.

Raw Score	Scaled Score	Percentile Rank
98-101	180	99.9 %
97	179	99.9 %

96	178	99.9%
94-95	177	99.8%
93	176	99.6%
92	175	99.4%
91	174	99.2%
90	173	99.0%
88-89	172	98.6%
87	171	98.0%
86	170	97.4%
84-85	169	96.7%

83	168	95.9%
81-82	167	94.6%
80	166	93.2%
78-79	165	92.0%
77	164	90.0%
75-76	163	88.1%
73-74	162	85.9%
72	161	83.4%
70-71	160	80.4%
68-69	159	77.6%

67	158	74.6 %
65-66	157	70.9 %
63-64	156	67.4 %
61-62	155	63.9 %
60	154	59.7 %
58-59	153	55.6 %
56-57	152	52.2 %
55	151	48.1 %

LSAT SCORES VS. GPA

While it varies between law schools, many admissions offices weigh your LSAT scores much more heavily than your GPA. Some law schools base 70% of their standard on your LSAT and 30% on your GPA.

Other schools create an index to evaluate each candidate. For example, they might use the equation (LSAT score - 120) + (GPA x 20). Meaning an LSAT score of 160 and a GPA of 3.5 would yield an admissions index of 110.

WHY LSAT SCORES ARE SO IMPORTANT

Some aspiring law students find it surprising or frustrating that their GPA is weighed so lightly in the admissions process. They worked hard over four years to achieve their GPA. And the LSAT is just one 3.5 hour test.

One reason law schools weigh LSAT scores more heavily is that GPAs at different schools require different levels of talent and hard work. Even at the same school, some classes are graded much more harshly than others. Two people with similar talent and hard work in the same major who took different courses may end up with very different GPAs.

While medical schools have a set of required undergrad courses for a student to be eligible, law schools accept students accept students from hundreds of majors who have taken thousands of different classes. So a standardized test helps them create a level playing field in the application process.

Another reason LSAT scores are weighed so heavily is that they don't consider references to be reliably objective. Many professors are pressured by their school to do whatever they can to help students get into top graduate programs. So applicants whose professors call them outstanding students do little to improve their candidacy.

Application essays are also unreliable since a number of admissions consulting programs help students write these kinds of essays. Many law schools don't even have the time or manpower to read all application essays. So applicants with low LSAT and GPA scores may never have their essays read by the admissions team. Therefore, the most effective and objective way to stand out as a law school applicant is to earn a high LSAT score.

The good news is that with the right amount of time, effort, and strategy, it is very possible to raise your LSAT score by 20-30%.

LSAT Sections

There are three types of scored, multiple choice LSAT sections, along with an unscored sample. The multiple choice sections are called Reading Comprehension, Logical Reasoning, and Analytical Reasoning.

LSAT Reading Comprehension is similar to the reading sections of other tests, including the SAT, ACT, GRE, and GMAT. You'll be given a passage that's about half a page long, and then you'll have a handful of questions to answer about that passage. There are three individual passages and one pair of passages (two shorter passages with a single set of questions asking you to compare the two) on each test. There are typically 27 questions on this section. Since there are roughly 100 scored questions on the entire exam, Reading

Comprehension is worth about 27% of your total score.

Logical Reasoning is probably something new for you unless you've taken the GMATand remember the Critical Reasoning component. In this section, you'll be given a short paragraph that poses an argument or lays out some facts, and then you'll be asked a single question about that paragraph. For example, you might be asked which answer choice strengthens the argument, weakens the argument, or provides an explanation of facts in the paragraph that seem to contradict each other. There are two Logical Reasoning is worth about 50% of your total LSAT score.

The Analytical Reasoning section better known as Logical Games - is the most notorious section of the exam. It intimidates test takers because it's unlike what they're used to seeing on other standardized tests, but it's still quite learnable. It consists of four separate "games," in which you'll be given a scenario and a set of rules, and you have to answer questions about possible outcomes. For example, you might be asked to arrange the order in which seven planes land at an airport terminal, but you'll only be given basics like. "If Plane P arrives before Plane S or Plane T, then it must also arrive after Plane X." Once you familiarize yourself with the most common game types, these can actually be kind of fun! In any case, there is only one Logic Games section and it usually only has about 23 questions, so it's only worth about 23% of your score.

Finally, there's the writing sample. The writing sample is the final stage of the exam, and it's unscored. However your entire writing sample will be sent with your score when you apply to law school, so you don't want to forget about this section, You'll be given a scenario and asked to make a choice between two courses of action. There will be a few criteria provided to help you make your decision, and all you have to do is make a strong argument in support of your course of action. No prior knowledge of the topic is required or expected, and there is no right or wrong answer. Basically, this is your chance to show off your ability to argue a point, and since you'll be doing a lot of that in law school, this is also a great way to test the waters.

When to Start Prepping for the LSATS

It is recommended that you start your LSAT prep about 5 to 6 months before you plan on taking the exam. Beginning in 2019, the LSAT is offered 9 times per year, so no matter when you want to take the test, NOW is a good time to start studying. So, for example, if you plan on taking the June LSAT, then ideally you should start thinking about preparing for the LSAT as early as the preceding December or January.

About 6 months before test day, you should take a timed, practice LSAT preptest in order to get a baseline score that you will spend the next 6 months working your way up from. See How to start preparing for the LSAT for more tips. Also, you will need some Real LSAT preptests to work on.

If you start 6 months in advance, you don't need to spend every day on LSAT prep. However, starting this early is an advantage, because even if you only spend a few hours every weekend for the first 3 months, you will have more time to familiarize yourself with the LSAT. A big part of mastering the LSAT is simply becoming familiar and comfortable with the material.

The last 3 months before the LSAT will be the most important. During this period, you should really step up your LSAT prep. Dedicate at least 10-20 hours a week studying and reviewing the best lsat prep books and working through practice test questions.

During the final few weeks before you take the LSAT, you should clear your schedule of everything except for preparing for the LSAT.

When to Take the LSAT

The LSAT is offered four times a year, in January/February, June, September/October, and November/December.

The exam is typically administered worldwide on the first Saturday of the month (or the last Saturday in September), but there are a few exceptions:

- The June administration is usually on the first Monday of the month.
- A weekday option exclusively for Sabbath observes is paired with each Saturday administration. It usually takes place on Monday, Tuesday, or Wednesday after the regular Saturday date.

- Administration in Asia, Australia, and New Zealand are typically on the last Sunday of February and June, and there are accordingly no separate administrations for Sabbath observers in those regions.
- There is a Spanish LSAT offered once per year at two test centers in Puerto Rico. This exam is only intended for students applying to law schools in Puerto Rico.

The good news is you have many LSAT test dates to choose from - you just have to narrow down which option is best for you. You'll want to consider when you're planning to apply to law school so you can ensure your LSAT scores will be available in time to apply. If you're not sure when you want to start law school, you have a little more flexibility. LSAT scores are valid for up to five (5) years, so you can take the test early and leave a cushion for retakes, work obligations, and other outside commitments.

June is one of the most popular test dates among students. For test takers who are currently still in undergrad, it falls over summer break, so June represents a rare opportunity to be able to study and take the test with fewer class and club responsibilities in the way. Keep in mind, however, that you'll likely have final exams and course commitments to balance until just a few weeks before the test date.

June is early enough that you can take the test and get your scores back in time to apply early in the admissions cycle that same year. You'll have the rest of your summer to pull together letters of recommendation, personal statements, and resumes without burdening yourself with logic games. Even if you later decide your June score is too low and requires a retake, retaking the September/October test still puts you on the early end of the application cycle.

Since June is also the only test that the LSAT administered in the afternoon, it's the perfect choice for those of you who definitely aren't morning people. That's right: There's no need to fear oversleeping or killing your score with too much of a caffeine buzz.

One of the benefits of the September/October test date is that it gives you the entire summer to study, which is particularly advantageous for current undergraduates. However, remember that those pesky fall semester classes will have started up again by September, so if you're still in school, you'll have more commitments on your plate. If you're worried about getting rusty on the LSAT skills you picked up over the summer, keep up with the study schedule as much as you can, even in the midst of homework and other tests.

The downside to taking your first LSAT around this time is that you'll really want to nail this test if you plan to apply early in the admissions cycle. Getting a golden LSAT score from this test date is ideal because it will still allow you to apply about as early as all of the students who sat from the June LSAT. If you're not satisfied with your score in September/October, you'll have to wait until December to retake, which takes you out of the running for an early admissions review.

The November/December LSAT will be the last chance you'll have to take the LSAT and still be considered for the current admissions cycle to top law schools. You'll be applying late in the cycle with a score from a December test, but you'll still be on time if you make sure other parts of your application (like your resume and personal statement) are ready to go. Keep this point in mind, especially if you're flip-flopping about how ready you are for the September/October test.

Some students intentionally impose a September/ October test date on themselves, even if that's unrealistic for them to achieve a good score. Remember that every single law school will accept your December score. Be sure to give yourself enough time to do your best.

The January/February LSAT is great for eager students applying in the following application cycle - it can take a lot of stress off your mind to know that you have many opportunities to retake and many more months to study and prepare your applications, if needed.

However, the January/February LSAT would be less than ideal for students interested in matriculating that same year. A number of school won't consider a student with a January or February LSAT score in an applicant pool for that same year. And while it's true that many schools will still consider such a student, you'd still be applying on the very late end of the application timeline.

The first March LSAT will be offered in March 2018. Like the February LSAT, the March LSAT is a great choice for students who are looking to get the LSAT out of the way early and have time to focus on other parts of the law school application. However, it's not a good choice if you're hoping to start law school the same year, because you'll get the results back too late to apply to most schools. So, only consider the March LSAT if you're hoping to get the

LSAT done early in the application process and have time to retest/retake if needed.

The most important thing is to choose a date that you will be best prepared for. It's stressful to be rounding the corner of your test date only to realize that you're 10 points from where you want to be scoring. While there are pros and cons to each of the test dates on the calendar, no consideration outweighs a fantastic score (even if that score means applying later in the application cycle).

Your performance in the LSAT exam is based on how well you scored in the four multiple-choice sections:

- Reading Comprehension
- Analytical Reasoning
- Logical Reasoning (2 sections)

There is another section which is unscored as it's a trial section meant for research to determine the psychometric data on the consistency of the test. The Writing Sample also doesn't contribute to the final score as it's unscored.

There are about 100 questions distributed among the four scored sections, and each is allotted one point each. There is no bias with any section as the score is the same for all the sections.
You get a point for each correctly answered question, and no point is given for wrongly answered question; no negative point allocation or partial score.
So, it's imperative that you answer all questions as best as you can and attempt all questions if time permits.

The number of answered correctly answered multiple choice questions is your raw score. Once this score is known, it's easy to calculate the total score through a conversion table. The conversion table for each test is posted by LSAC and can be accessed on lsat.magoosh.com. Although each tests conversion table is slightly different, they have a relatively consistent number. LSAC uploads your raw score into a very complicated algorithm known as equating which factor in your test difficulty as against the previous tests and total questions. Below is an example of a conversion table created by finding the average of the 15 most recent LSAT conversion tables for a robust and reliable estimate.

Three Month Study Schedule Studying for the LSAT

Ideally, students should use between 3 to 6 months for LSAT preparation, and with three months you need to start now! There are a number of three Month Study Plans that provide you with ideas of where to focus on and prepare you well for every aspect of the LSAT.

Two Month Study Schedule

The LSAT requires an excellent study plan due to its difficulty level. But some students plan to prepare for the exam within less period. It is not usually recommended that students to rush things, but some people are well suited to this type of preparation.

One Month Study Schedule

Though one month schedule is not advisable for LSAT preparation but it happens. There are students who plan to write LSAT with no effective study plan. However, with the ideal plan coupled with hard work, we believe you can pull through and pass LSAT within a month study.

Two-Week (16-Day) Study Schedule
To prepare adequately for LSAT, you will need more than two weeks ideally, but if that's all you've got you need to start your preparation today! Your extremely low preparation time could be as a result of an unplanned event such as purchasing of unhelpful prep materials. But, if you want to improve your score within this short period, then you should focus your attention on reading this plan.

LSAT Study Strategies

Ultimately, LSAT study guide is about building new habits, and that doesn't happen quickly. If you're doing things right, you'll feel off-balance in the first phase of the preparation because you're learning entirely new approaches to the exam. As you move into the second phase, you'll feel more comfortable with the process, but you might feel impatient with the results. This is because you've learned a good approach to the test, but you haven't mastered it yet. It's like playing a game in which you know all the rules and you're always exactly where you should be, but you keep dropping the ball. In the third phase, you finally start to master the test. This is where you focus on small adjustments to your technique, each of which may take time to perfect and might only result in one or two more correct answers.

Regardless of the phase you're currently in, process may feel slow. Don't focus on how you're scoring today vs last week. Instead, try to focus on where you started, how far you've come, and what you can do next to get closer to your goal.

There are four components to an effective LSAT study program: (1) full-length, timed practice tests; (2) individual, timed practice sections; (3) an error log; and (4) untimed, targeted practice.

Full-Length, Timed Practice Tests

This is a great starting point of your LSAT test preparation. We recommend taking a full-length practice test before you watch an online lesson or attend your first preparation class. That way, you get a realistic idea of where you're starting out, and you can set reasonable goals for how far you'll progress.

After your first practice test, strike a balance between further practice tests and the other three elements of effective LSAT test preparation. Taking weekly practice tests is probably overkill, but avoiding them entirely is also unwise. Over-testing can exhaust you while reinforcing bad habits and taking up time that could be spent learning.

It's like an endless scrimmaging without any practice or coaching in between. On the other hand, under-testing leaves you vulnerable to test day surprises like fatigue or poor planning (timing bathroom breaks, packing good quality snacks, etc.). In other words, it's like playing catch every day, and then thinking you're ready for your first baseball game.

Instead, aim to complete one full-length, timed practice test after every 2-4 tests' worth of material you complete as either individual, timed sections or untimed, targeted practice. If you work on LSAT preparation 3-4 days per week for 30-60 minutes per day, you'll be ready for a practice test every 2-3 weeks.

Individual, Timed Practice Sections

This just means sitting down, setting a timer for 35 minutes, and completing one section on an LSAT from start to finish.

I recommend doing this about 3 times per week (one for each LSAT section type). Just make sure to leave room for regular untimed, targeted practice. For example, don't do 4 or 5 Logic games practice sections in a row without doing some targeted Logic Games practice in between to analyze your progress.

The key to doing timed practice sections is making them as authentic as possible. Even though you're only completing one section, treat it like the real thing. Find a quiet space where you'll be undisturbed. Use a pencil. If you finish early, use the remaining time to double check your answers. If you're running out of time, guess on the remaining questions and circle them to keep track of where you guessed. Apply your pacing strategies accurately, and don't cheat by stopping the clock for a break.

When you're done with a section, score it, record any mistakes in your error log, and put it away. You'll look at it again during your untimed, targeted practice.

Error Log

Any time you take a full-length practice test or complete a timed practice section, score it right away and enter it into your error log. It's important to do this immediately afterward because the questions are still fresh in your mind and you'll remember more of the reasoning behind your answers.

For each question you missed, record the following in your error log.

1. The PreTest, section, and question number (so you can find it again later)
2. 2. The question type (for example, Inference, Assumption, Parallel Reasoning, etc.)
3. 3. The correct answer choice
4. The incorrect answer choice that you selected
5. Your best description of the mistake you made (misinterpreted something, picked an answer choice that was too extreme, confused the premise and the conclusion, etc.)

Once you've completed your error log, put away your LSAT prep for the day and relax. You've recorded what you need to know for the future, so it won't be forgotten.

<u>Untimed, Targeted Practice</u>

Follow up on every timed practice test or practice section with some untimed, targeted practice. That doesn't mean you have to do targeted after every, single practice section you complete. Instead, you could target Logical Reasoning one day by reviewing the last 2 or 3 timed LR sections you completed and doing a few new LR questions untimed.

To make the most of your targeted practice:

Focus on just one section type each time you do targeted practice

Look at your most recent error log entries. Is there a question type or mistake you've been struggling with a lot lately?

If it's a question type, review lessons on that question type and then search for a handful of them to complete slowly and methodically. Don't answer until you feel very confident that you understand the question and all the answer choices.

If it's a particular mistake you're making frequently, or if your errors vary a lot, try an untimed practice section in which you focus on identifying and avoiding that mistake or other trap answer choices.

Section Strategies

There are four major sections in the LSAT exam, with each section having a specific time limit. So, this gives students a feeling of taking three separate tests to get an LSAT score. While you plan for the test, ensure you pass all three sections excellently. Scoring low on a particular section will affect your score significantly.

Analytical Reasoning

Another name for this section is the Logic Games, and most feel it the toughest in the LSAT exam. Most people don't have an idea of how best to handle this test section. However, it has been proved that with proper preparation and orientation about this test, it's not as tough as people portray it to be. It's the easiest to learn section of the entire exam, and if well handled can boost a candidate's overall score.

This section comprises of some "games," which is centered around everyday tasks like cloth matching, team picking, class schedule, etc. It also contains a set of rules to restrict the ways a game can be solved. For instance, you must include two females in your team, or you can't take Physics before Chemistry). It will usually be followed with a set of five to seven questions, asking you to decide on both possible and impossible outcomes.

The test also comprises of one Analytical Reasoning section and four games. Recently, the analytical reasoning section has modified with 23 questions. The questions are arranged in no special order of difficulty.

Though, one thing to be sure about is that the four games come in different difficulty level. Some are extremely difficult, while others are quite easy. This section adds 23% to your total score.

In most tests, you need to understand how to prepare adequately with all the knowledge you have acquired. Indeed, this is what reasoning testis about, and our study guide will help to enhance your LSAT analytical reasoning skills

Questions related to Analytical Reasoning are aimed at assessing your ability to carefully analyze an important group of facts and rules at which truth could or will be established.

Analytical Reasoning questions are given in sets, and each of them addresses a single passage which is addressing a particular scenario. Some notable examples of the scenario used includes order or grouping relationships or both of them together. For instance, a question could consist of employees scheduled for work shifts, task order based on priority setting, assigning tutors to a section of the class, and distributing projects funds.

Usually, the specific scenarios attached to these questions don't have any relationship with the law because they are not set for law students alone.

However, Analytical Reasoning questions test skills that closely parallel those involved in determining what could or must be the case given a set of regulations, the terms of a contract, or the facts of a legal case in relation to the law.

In this sense, Analytical reasoning questions reflect the kinds of detailed analyses of relationships and sets of constraints that a law student must perform in legal problem solving. For example, an AR passage might describe six diplomats being seated around a table, following certain rules of protocol as to who can sit where. You might then be asked to answer questions about the logical implications of the rules as they apply to the scenario. For example, you might be asked who can sit between diplomats X and Y, or who cannot sit next to X if W sits next to Y.

Similarly, in law school you might be asked to analyze a scenario involving a set of particular circumstances and a set of rules that apply to the scenario—rules such as constitutional provisions, statutes, administrative codes, or prior rulings that have been upheld. You might then be asked to determine the legal options in the scenario: what is required given the scenario, what is permissible given the scenario, and what is prohibited given the scenario. Or you might be asked to develop a "theory" for the case: when faced with an incomplete set of facts about the case, you must fill in the picture based on what is implied by the facts that are known. Sometimes you will be asked to assess the impact of hypotheticals that add new information (as in the example above: If W sits next to Y, then who cannot sit next to X.).

Analytical Reasoning questions test a range of deductive reasoning skills:

Comprehending the basic structure of a set of relationships by determining a complete solution to the problem posed (for example, an acceptable seating arrangement of all six diplomats around a table)

Reasoning with conditional ("if-then") statements

Inferring what could be true or must be true from given facts and rules

Inferring what could be true or must be true from given facts and rules together with new information presented in hypotheticals

Recognizing when two statements are logically equivalent in context

You don't need any formal training in logic to answer these questions correctly. AR questions are intended to be answered using knowledge, skills, and reasoning ability generally expected of college students and graduates.

Steps to Take and Questions to Ask

What is an argument?

A strong argument tries to persuade the reader to accept a point of view using:
1. A declarative statement of an idea or opinion.

2. Support for the statement: including relevant facts, opinions based on facts and/or careful reasoning.

What is the Analysis of Argument?

Analysis of Argument questions present a short argument on an issue where you discuss how well it is reasoned.

Here is an example of an Analysis of Argument question:

Toads cause warts. I touched a toad last week and now I have a wart; therefore the toad was responsible.

How would you rate the accuracy of the above statement? Support your position with reasons and examples.

Consider the following example:

Stimulus: *Toads cause warts. I touched a toad last week and now I have a wart; therefore, the toad was responsible.*

Question Stem: *How would you rate the accuracy of the above statement? Support your position with reasons and examples.*

The Stimulus

In the first part of the Analysis of Argument topic, the writer tries to persuade you of his conclusion by referring to evidence. Be on the lookout for assumptions and poor logical reasoning used to come to the conclusion.

The Question Stem

Question stems will ask you to explain why an argument is not convincing, and discuss improvements to the argument. For this task, you'll need to first analyze the argument itself and evaluate its use of evidence. Second, you'll need to explain how a different approach or more information would make the argument itself better (or possibly worse).

They say: Explain what, if anything, would make the argument more valid and convincing or help you to better evaluate its conclusion.

LSAT Writing Sample Essay Guidelines and Tips

Attack the Argument

Each argument's stimulus has been intentionally "loaded" with flaws or fallacies that you should acknowledge and discuss. If you fail to see the fundamental problems in the argument, you will not get a high score. Attacking questions with logic means addressing the thought process outlined in the prompt rather than its background or setup information, details presented as fact.

The purpose of the essay is for you to critique the reasoning in the argument. Your personal opinions are not relevant. Instead, your essay needs to focus on flaws in the argument and how the argument could be strengthened.

Taking a Stance Quiz 1: Analysis of Argument

Example

Prompt:

"The temperature in Smithtown averages ten degrees hotter than the temperature in Jonestown during the summer. Numerous studies, meanwhile, confirm a direct link between temperature and thirst. As such, one can expect residents of Smithtown to consume more water than residents of Jonestown."

A. "It may be true that residents of Smithtown consume more water than those of Jonestown due to increased summer temperatures, but it is not wise to trust this assertion without knowing more information, such as the duration of the temperature comparisons. It is possible, for example, that the temperature study was conducted during a single odd summer in which one city had higher temperatures—when the two cities had equal temperatures every other year. If this is the case, then water consumption is likely to remain equal."

-Incorrect: The temperature differences are presented as facts and not indicative of the author's thought process. An attack on logic would address the conclusion drawn from these temperatures.

B. "While the prompt appears credible at first due to its citation of 'numerous studies', it is essential to remember that not all studies are equal. If the studies are dated or linked to unreliable scientists or equipment, then their findings might be wholly inaccurate—and therein have no correlation with the level of thirst in these two towns despite even larger temperature differences."

-Incorrect: This focuses on studies that have been presented as fact, not opinion. An attack on logic would address the conclusion drawn from these temperatures: that they will ultimately lead to increased water consumption in the hotter town.

C. "I disagree with the prompt, as it ignores other alternatives that residents of Smithtown might use to cope with the increased heat, such using more air conditioning to lower temperatures (which, according to the prompt, would decrease thirst) or quenching their increased thirst with sports drinks rather than water."

-Correct! - This focuses on the author's use of logic to conclude that residents in the hotter area will use water to quench their thirst rather than using technology to lower the temperature (and the related level of thirst) or another liquid to fulfill their thirst. The studies and statistics mentioned in the prompt should be accepted as fact, as they exist only to create a platform to showcase the author's logic.

Creating Content

Once you've identified the proper stance, you must support this stance in your body section using clear examples.
There are two basic types of examples, both of which you must master to succeed:
1) The Real-World Example:
This type of example is drawn from your personal readings and experience.
To develop strong personal examples, your examples must extend outward from their singular nature and should represent universal trends rather than isolated incidents.
2) The Theoretical Example:
This type of example is wholly imaginary and created by you for the sole purpose of supporting or opposing the prompt.
To develop strong hypothetical examples, your examples must remain grounded in reality, meaning that they must still remain logical, plausible, and relevant to the prompt.

<u>Creating Content Analysis of Issue Examples 1</u>

Prompt:
"In business, it takes a lot of money to make a lot of money."

A. "Since Steve Jobs returned to Apple as its CEO, he has significantly grown its market share and profits by reimagining its products. However, this required billions of dollars and would not have been possible had Apple not already had such capital."

-Correct! - This highlights a universal truth that most businesses have to spend money in order to make money by investing in products, infrastructure, and personnel.

B. "An entrepreneur can easily take out a loan to pay for his company's startup costs, spending a bank's money rather than his own. This would mean he was not spending money in order to make money."
-Incorrect- This is a specific example but illogically ignores the fact that money is still being spent, as the entrepreneur would be spending the bank's money (in addition to a probable down payment on this loan and eventual monthly payments).

C. . "Many of the best performing investment funds have high minimum buy-in fees, meaning their potential reward is only available to those wealthy enough to afford such minimums."
- Correct! - This focuses on a trend across many_funds rather than a specific fund, which would fail to universally address the prompt.

D. "A person with a potentially profitable idea, such as founding the next big fast food chain, will need money to build this idea—money to purchase land, pay for food supplies, hire and train workers, and hire lawyers to protect these assets."
-Correct! - This theoretical example focuses on costs that will apply to many types of businesses, not just fast food establishments. This proves a need for initial capital across the board.

Creating Content Analysis of Examples 2

A. "While space travel is currently very expensive, it remains a strong investment because money spent today will make space travel cheaper in the future. Building the space station, for example, was quite expensive; however, its construction was a one-time expense. The more it is used, the more it will pay for itself—and in the future, it will require only maintenance expenses rather than construction expenses, which will be much more affordable."
-Correct! - This stays parallel by addressing current expenses, but uses logic to explain why these expenses will ultimately prove to be a worthy investment.

B. "While space travel might not bring back tangible profit from outer space, such as gold and minerals, the pursuit of such has yielded great technological benefits, such as the development of foams and safety equipment that continues to make its way into the lives of ordinary civilians."
-Correct - Financial benefits are not the only reward on an investment. Technological benefits and innovations count as well.

C."It is theorized that alternative energies such as hydrogen will one day be able to power spacecraft for a fraction of the price of fossil fuels."
-Incorrect- This is a theory, not a fact, and it addresses future expenses rather than the current expenses targeted in the prompt.

D. "The first space shuttle launched into space cost taxpayers more than a billion dollars."
-Incorrect - This focuses on past expenses rather than current expenses.

Creating a Strong Argument

Consider the following example:
"It's going to snow tomorrow, so the university should cancel classes."
While this example may seem complete, it is missing a supporting link between the claim ("the university should cancel classes") and the evidence ("it's going to snow tomorrow").
Notice the improvement after supporting points are added:
"It's going to snow tomorrow, which will make the roads slick and dangerous. To avoid injuries to commuting students and faculty, the university should cancel classes until the roads are safe again."
<u>Strengthening Arguments Example 1</u>

Prompt: "Toads cause warts. I touched a toad last week and now I have a wart;
therefore, the toad was responsible."

A. "Similarly, it is important to know the author's history with warts and toads. If, for example, the author has never before touched a toad but has developed warts on a weekly basis, then it is likely that the wart is caused by other reasons, such as a chronic virus such as the human papilloma virus that causes warts to appear regardless of external contact."
-Correct - Adding the example of an internal virus explains why it is important to know the author's relevant background, as the new wart might have appeared due to a preexisting condition.

B. "It is possible that this particular toad was not a carrier of the bacteria or virus that causes warts. The best way to know would be to find the toad and conduct a scientific test to determine whether or not the wart-causing catalyst was present."
-Incorrect - This is sound advice, but not appropriate for an analysis essay as it fails to address the author's conclusion from the information given. Rather than pointing out the best way to arrive at a separate conclusion, a stronger example would analyze the logic the author used to arrive at the present conclusion.

C. "Toads may cause warts, but more information is needed to link this particular wart with the toad. For example, it is important to know where the warts developed and what body part or parts came into contact with the toad."
-Incorrect - "This fails to explain why it is important to know this information. A stronger example would explain that warts are spread through direct contact, then highlight the potential absence of direct contact if the wart appeared on the author's wrist when the author only touched the toad with his or her foot."

Finding Errors

There are seven logical errors that commonly appear in the essay questions. When writing your essay argument, explicitly identify the logical flaws. These flaws also tend to occur in the critical reasoning section of the Verbal LSAT, so your preparation here will benefit you when taking that section.

Circular Reasoning

Here, an unsubstantiated assertion is used to justify another unsubstantiated assertion, which is used to justify the first statement. For instance, Joe and Fred show up at an exclusive club. When asked if they are members, Joe says "I'll vouch for Fred". When Joe is asked for evidence that he's a member, Fred says, "I'll vouch for him".

Fallacy of the Insufficient Sample

The *Fallacy of the Insufficient Sample* is committed whenever an inadequate sample is used to justify the conclusion drawn.

The following argument commits a *Fallacy of the Insufficient Sample*:

I have worked with three people from New York City and found them to be obnoxious, pushy and rude. It is obvious that people from New York City have a bad attitude.

The data for the inference in this argument are insufficient to support the conclusion. Three observations of three people are not sufficient to support a conclusion about the entire population of a city.

The Fallacy of the Biased Sample

The *Fallacy of the Biased Sample* is committed whenever the data for a statistical inference is drawn from a sample that is not representative of the population under consideration. The data used to make a generalization are drawn from a group that does not represent the whole.

The following argument commits a *Fallacy of the Biased Sample*:

In a recent survey conducted by Wall Street Weekly, 80% of the respondents indicated their strong disapproval of increased capital gains taxes. This survey clearly shows that increased capital gains taxes will meet with strong opposition from the electorate.

The data for the inference in this argument are drawn from a sample that is not representative of the entire electorate. Since the survey was conducted on people who invest, not all members of the electorate have an equal chance of being included in the sample. Moreover, people who read about investing are more likely to have an opinion on the topic of taxes on investments that differs from the opinion of the population at large.

Straw Man

Here, the speaker attributes an argument to an opponent, and that argument does not represent the opponent's true position. For instance, a political candidate might charge that his opponent "wants to let all prisoners go free", when in fact his opponent simply favors a highly limited furlough system. The person is portrayed as someone he is not.

Ad hominem

One of the most often-employed fallacies, ad hominem means “to the man” and indicates an attack made on a person rather than on the statements that person has made. An example is: “Don’t listen to my opponent, he’s a homosexual.”

Fallacy of Faulty Analogy

Reasoning by analogy makes an unsubstantiated assumption when comparing two similar things. The fallacy of faulty analogy assumes that since two things are alike in many ways, they will share other traits in common. *Faulty Analogy*arguments conclude that one similarity results in another, when in fact, there can be no way of inferring this extra similarity.

The following is an example of a *Fallacy of Faulty Analogy*:
Ted and Jim excel at both football and basketball. Since Ted is also a track star, Jim likely also excels at track.
In this example, numerous similarities between Ted and Jim are taken as the basis for the inference that they share additional traits.

The “After This, Therefore, Because of This” Fallacy (Post hoc ergo propter hoc)

This is a “false cause” fallacy in which something is associated with something else because of mere proximity of time. One often encounters, such as in news stories, people assuming that because one thing happened after another, the first caused it, as with, “I touched a toad; I have a wart; the toad caused the wart.” The error in the arguments that commit this fallacy is that their conclusions are

simply claims and are insufficiently substantiated by the evidence.
Here are two examples of the *After This, Therefore Because of This* Fallacy:

Ten minutes after walking into the auditorium, I began to feel sick to
my stomach. There must have been something in the air in that building that caused my nausea.

The stock market declined shortly after the election of the president,
thus indicating the lack of confidence the business community has in the new administration.

In the first example, a causal connection is posited between two events simply on the basis of one occurring before the other. Without further evidence to support it, the causal claim based on the correlation is premature.
The second example is typical of modern news reporting. The only evidence offered in this argument to support the implicit causal claim that the decline in the stock market was caused by the election of the president is that the election preceded the decline. While this may have been a causal factor in the decline of the stock market, to argue that it is the main cause without additional information is to commit the *After This, Therefore, Because of This* Fallacy.

The "All Things are Equal" Fallacy

This fallacy is committed when background conditions are assumed, without justification, to have remained the same at different times/ locations. In most instances, this is an unwarranted assumption for the simple reason that things rarely remain the same over extended periods, and things rarely remain the same from place to place.

The last Democratic Party winner of the New Hampshire primary won the general election. This year, the winner of the New Hampshire primary will win the general election.
The assumption operative in this argument is that nothing has changed since the last primary. No evidence or justification is offered for this assumption.

The Either-Or Thinking

This is the so-called black-or-white fallacy. Essentially it says, "Either you believe what I'm saying or you must believe exactly the opposite." Here is an example of the black-or-white fallacy: *Since you don't believe that the earth is teetering on the edge of destruction, you must believe that pollution and other adverse effects that man has on the environment are of no concern whatsoever.* The argument above assumes that only two possible alternatives are open to us. There is no room for a middle ground.

Non Sequitur
This means "does not follow," which is short for: the conclusion does not follow from the premise. To say, "The house is white; therefore, it must be big" is an example. The house may be big but there is no intrinsic connection with its being white.

Argument ad populum
A group of kindergartners is studying a frog, trying to determine its sex. "I wonder if it's a boy frog or a girl frog," says one student. "I know how we can tell!" pipes up another. "All right, how?" asks the

teacher, resigned to the worst. Beams the child: "We can vote."

This is *argumentum ad populum*, the belief that truth can be determined by more or less putting it to a vote. Democracy is a very nice thing, but it doesn't determine truth. Polls are good for telling you what people think, not whether those thoughts are correct.

How to solve this section:

Your first line of action is to identify the various types of game available. Practically, all the games can be directly used for any of the seven major LSAT categories. However, correctly identifying each category question will pose a significant challenge.

Once this can be sorted and you correctly know the type of game, a diagram can be set up immediately, and the information supplied.

The result needs to be carefully spotted and analyzed throughout the remaining part of the game. Once the diagram has been set up, all you have left is to use it alongside your result to answer the ensuing questions.

Logical Reasoning

In the Logical Reasoning section, every question is linked with a short stimulus (a set of fact or argument). This section comprises of several types of question which is associated with one out of the following skills: recognizing passive assumptions in arguments, drawing valid inferences based on facts supplied, or rightly analyzing an argument structure.

The LSAT comprises of two Logical Reasoning sections, each containing 25 questions. You will most likely not come across two questions per stimulus, but you may encounter two questions in a row associated with the same stimulus. As you answer the question, the difficulty level increases, and it tends to get relaxed as you approach the end. This section carries about 50% of the entire exam score.

Aside from having an excellent reasoning ability, you ought to also know how to utilize some specific non-legal terms for you to excel in this test. Understand these terms and their use in a testing situation such as the LSAT. Our study guide is available to serve as a point this out to you.

As you are already aware that arguments are an integral aspect of the law, and it also forms an essential part of legal analysis. Law school teachings is predicated based on critical reasoning skills. As you are already aware that arguments are an integral aspect of the law, and it also forms an integral part of legal analysis. Law school teachings is predicated based on critical reasoning skills. As a student of law, you are required to utilize all the skills at your disposal, such as evaluating, analyzing, refuting, and constructing arguments.

Relevant information should be easily identified in an argument as you analyze what difference more evidence could make. You will also be required to know how to combine an opposing line of thought while you persuade others with your arguments.

The question set in the Logical Reasoning section is aimed at evaluating your ability to analyze,

examine, and to assess arguments thoroughly as they appear in everyday communication.
These questions come from short arguments culled from several sources, both informally and formally such as newspapers, publications, adverts, and magazines. These short arguments pattern is identical to those in legal reasoning and complexity, although some of the arguments have law as their main subject.

To solve any Logical Reasoning question, a short passage will be given which need to read and understand before proceeding to answer one question or two (in the rare case). The questions are specially set to test a vast range of skills utilized in critical thinking, with a significant focus on critical legal reasoning skills.

Some of the critical legal reasoning skills include:

- Recognizing argument parts as well as their relationships
- Recognizing discrepancies or disagreed points
- Discovering assumptions made in specific arguments
- Deducing conclusion from well-supported arguments
- Identifying similarities and differences among a line of thought
- Understanding the impact additional evidence will make in an argument
- Analogic Reasoning
- Spotting flaws in arguments
- Recognizing and applying rules or principles or rules
- Identifying explanations

You don't need to know so much about logical terminologies before you can answer Logical Reasoning questions. For instance, there are specific terms like "syllogism" or "ad hominem," which you need to understand their meaning. However, you will be required to understand and give a critical thought on the argument in the text.

To achieve this, it's imperative to have a thorough understanding of assumptions, arguments, premise, and conclusion which are all concepts in Logical Reasoning. You should make it a priority getting acquainted with these concepts.

<u>How to solve this section:</u>

This section comprises of a voluminous text which needs careful reading. There are several types of logical errors littered around the passages. LSAT Courses is designed to teach students the rudiments of logical reasoning as it also helps to identify common mistakes. With this, students can quickly identify logical errors in LSAT test arguments as well as future arguments in the law school.

The next step is to know the category of questions asked and the way they are phrased. Those who have done LSAT practice previously can attest that it's quite frustrating when you need to identify logical errors and still get a wrong answer due to misunderstanding the question.
To assist you in this aspect, we further explain the five main type of question so one can easily understand the way to answer each question.

Finally, create a plan of attack. You will be given a four-step process that will help you pick out the logical errors, understand the type of questions, and choose the best answer from the multiple choices.

Logical Reasoning Tests Reasoning Ability

Logical Reasoning questions are also designed to test your reasoning ability—that is, your ability to judge or form an opinion about the information you are given in the stimulus. By far the most important reasoning relationships for us to judge are those that exist between a point and the support given for that point in an argument.

Let's imagine some different ways they could test our ability to evaluate this relationship within arguments. Perhaps they could sometimes give us arguments that are valid—arguments for which the reasoning does justify the conclusion—and sometimes give us arguments that are not valid, and they could test our ability to decipher which ones are valid and which ones are not. Other questions could be set up much as a case is presented to a jury—we would be given a set of facts, and it would be up to us to determine whether the information proves the conclusion, doesn't prove it, or presents some sort of deadlock.

It's important to know that neither of these scenarios actually represent what will be asked of you on the LSAT.

When we are asked to evaluate the reasoning in an argument, it is always in terms of a very specific task: our job is to always evaluate and understand why the reasons given do not justify the point that is made. For every one of these questions, your understanding of why the support doesn't justify the conclusion will be your primary gauge for evaluating right and wrong answers.

Logical Reasoning problems do not ever require you to differentiate between valid and invalid reasoning within arguments. Instead, they test your ability to see, in a very specific way, why arguments are not valid. If you are good at this, you will be good at solving Logical Reasoning problems.

Logical Reasoning Tests Mental Discipline

We can define mental discipline as the ability to stay focused on the specific task at hand. Success on the LSAT requires extreme mental discipline, and the test is down right cruel to those who don't have it.

In terms of developing mental discipline, we give ourselves a huge head start when we have a clear understanding of the job, and of the best way to achieve it. But mental discipline takes far more than knowing. It requires sticking to that task—focusing on the argument, rather than the confusing background information, strengthening or weakening that argument, rather than just the point being made, not jumping to conclusions or forming opinions when the questions specifically ask for you not to judge, and remembering exactly what you are looking for in the right answer as you eliminate the wrong ones. Your mental discipline is a fairly good representation of the power of your brain, just like the ability to lift a certain amount of weight is a fairly good representation of the power in your arms. Exercising those arm muscles is the best way to develop their strength; working questions correctly, over and over again, is the best way to develop mental discipline.

Reading Comprehension

This section comes with passages from articles, essays, books, etc., with multiple choice questions after the passages. Typically, you will be asked to assess the purpose of the passage, its main idea, tone, or structure. You might also be tasked to analyze and relate the thinking pattern of various characters within the passage. The Reading Comprehension section is only one, and it's usually made up of 27 questions. Three distinct passages are given with questions underneath each of them; one pair of passages is also given with a set of questions for the pair. The three single passages and the paired ones are quite similar; however, their line of question is different, and one needs to identify points of agreement and divergence. It's interesting to note that this section carries about 27% of the total exam score.

So, what exactly are the reading comprehension skills needed to excel in this part of the LSAT? You will find that this test is more complicated than other reading comprehension tests, but in our guide, you will find out how to effectively study for it.

Both law school and the practice of law revolve around extensive reading of highly varied, dense, argumentative, and expository texts (for example, cases, codes, contracts, briefs, decisions, evidence). This reading must be exacting, distinguishing precisely what is said from what is not said. It involves comparison, analysis, synthesis, and application (for example, of principles and rules). It involves drawing appropriate inferences and applying ideas and arguments to new contexts. Law school reading also requires the ability to grasp unfamiliar subject matter and the ability to penetrate difficult and challenging material.

The purpose of LSAT Reading Comprehension questions is to measure the ability to read, with understanding and insight, examples of lengthy and complex materials similar to those commonly encountered in law school. The Reading Comprehension section of the LSAT contains four sets of reading questions, each set consisting of a selection of reading material followed by five to eight questions. The reading selection in three of the four sets consists of a single reading passage; the other set contains two related shorter passages. Sets with two passages are a variant of Reading Comprehension called Comparative Reading, which was introduced in June 2007.

Comparative Reading questions concern the relationship between the two passages, such as those of generalization/instance, principle/application, or point/counterpoint. Law school work often requires reading two or more texts in conjunction with each other and understanding their relationships. For example, a law student may read a trial court decision together with an appellate court decision that overturned it, or identify the fact pattern from a hypothetical suit together with the potentially controlling case law.

Reading selections for LSAT Reading Comprehension questions are drawn from a wide range of subjects in the humanities, the social sciences, the biological and physical sciences, and areas related to the law. Generally, the selections are densely written, use high-level vocabulary, and contain sophisticated argument or complex rhetorical structure (for example, multiple points of view). Reading Comprehension questions require you to read carefully and accurately, to determine the relationships among the various parts of the reading selection, and to draw reasonable inferences from the material in the selection. The questions may ask about the following characteristics of a passage or pair of passages:

- The main idea or primary purpose
- Information that is explicitly stated
- Information or ideas that can be inferred
- The meaning or purpose of words or phrases as used in context
- The organization or structure
- The application of information in the selection to a new context
- Principles that function in the selection
- Analogies to claims or arguments in the selection
- An author's attitude as revealed in the tone of a passage or the language used
- The impact of new information on claims or arguments in the selection

Perform these five steps while you read:

1. <u>Classify the Passage</u>

Is this passage persuasive or descriptive? Is it about science, business or humanities?

2. Analyze Paragraphs
Break down each paragraph. Look for the main idea, tone and transitions.

3. Identify Organization
Make a road map of the essay and/or draw an outline.

4. Find the Big Idea
Look for unusual language that makes an important point. Pay more attention to the first and last paragraphs.

5. Determine Purpose
Identify the conflicting perspectives within the essay, and the author's point-of-view.

To prepare for the questions, here are the 5 steps you should take while reading a passage.

1. Classify the Passage. Is it science or humanities? Is this a persuasive essay or a descriptive one?
2. Break Down Each Paragraph. Look for the tone, main idea, and transitions.
3. See the Organization. Make a road map of the essay and/or draw out a map structure on your scratch paper.
4. Find the Big Idea. Pay more attention to first and last paragraphs. Look for unusual language that makes an important point.
5. Diagnose the Author's Purpose. Look for intention in the essay.

Timing

We discussed some basic Reading Comprehension timing strategies back in Lesson 25.

Let's revisit some of the key points we made and discuss timing in more depth.

In recent years, every Reading Comprehension section has contained twenty-seven questions. This might change any minute, but it won't change drastically. In general, you want to spend about 2:30 to 3 minutes reading each passage and about 0:45 to a minute per question. Different questions will require varying amounts of time; however, most passages are of similar length, and once you settle into your practice exams, you should be able to set a fairly consistent reading pace.

Different test takers take different amounts of time initially reading a passage; people have been successful with a variety of strategies. In general, if you average more time (say, 4:00 or so) per read, you should expect to retain a bit more of the passage than what I typically suggest in the solutions, and you should expect that questions will go faster for you than I suggest. If you read faster than 2:30 or 3:00 per passage, you'll certainly have a bit more time for questions, but if you are reading at that fast of a pace, you want to make sure it's not putting you at risk for misunderstanding the main points or the reasoning structure.

We also discussed the fact that pace typically matches process—if your skills and habits are strong, timing becomes less of an issue. Timing is a more significant issue when your path to the right answer is less direct. Finally, we also discussed the fact that, when we have to make difficult decisions in terms of time, it's best to cut out individual questions rather than entire passages. We'll expand on both of those points in this lesson.

Basic Timing Instincts

Answering any LSAT question correctly involves a series of correct steps. These steps can overlap, and sometimes you can get away with not being "perfect" at one of them, but for every Reading Comprehension question, you will be required to

1) Understand the relevant information about the passage
2) Understand what the question stem is asking of you
3) See why the wrong answers are wrong
4) See why the right answer is right

The best way to think about the efficient use of time is to think about what you are doing relative to these necessary steps. Here's what I mean, in a bit more detail: It is an efficient use of time to stop during your read to think, when necessary, about the

reasoning structure of the passage. If you are certain that the second paragraph plays one role, but then, in reading the third paragraph, you are not so sure you understand the point of the passage at all, quickly go back and think about the second paragraph again. If you feel pretty certain about the two sides of an issue, but then something you read makes you feel like your priorities are out of whack, take the time to stop, reassess, and reread as necessary.

Of course, you can't spend an inordinate amount of time (to be discussed further in just a bit) doing this, but in general, this will be time well spent. The reason? Reasoning structure is always relevant to several of the questions you will see, and, as I'm sure many of you have experienced, it's next to impossible to get through the questions in an efficient manner if you don't have a good sense of reasoning structure.

It is commonly an inefficient use of time to stop during your read to think about the meaning of complex phrases or sentences. This is not true if that complex phrase or sentence is necessary for you to understand the central issue or a key opinion. However, in just about every other instance, you don't have to concern yourself with being perfectly
in tune with every detail mentioned.

Those random details are, mathematically speaking, unlikely to factor into any questions, and even if they do turn out to be relevant to a question, you can always come back to reread them as needed. If you find yourself rereading and rereading a sentence, ask yourself, do I understand why it is here? If you are not so clear on the what, but clear on the why, then move on and keep reading forward. It is always an efficient use of time to stop and carefully think about the question stem.

The question stem tells us a lot of things: it tells us what to expect from right answers
and, less directly, what to expect from wrong answers. It also tells us what we should

do—whether we should go back into the text to look at certain relevant information before looking at the answer choices, or whether we should move right into eliminating wrong choices.

It is an inefficient use of time (and an unnecessary distraction) to try to predict questions as you read, and it is an extremely inefficient use of your time to read the questions before you read the passage. Frankly, these strategies are so bad that I don't even want to bring them up, but I need to do so because they somehow exist in the general stratosphere of commonly used LSAT strategies. Do not read questions ahead of the passage, and do not try to anticipate questions as you read. These are both ineffective strategies for test takers at all score levels. You use time efficiently when you eliminate incorrect answers quickly and for concrete reasons.

You use your time Inefficiently when you eliminate when you are less than certain and commonly have to go back to answers you've already eliminated. There are definite reasons that answers are wrong, and the elimination process is about using these definite reasons to get rid of answers with confidence. Do not linger during the elimination process. If an answer seems wrong but you just can't put your finger on why, it may just be the right answer in disguise—leave it for after the elimination round. Your eliminations should be certain and quick, and you should never (or very, very rarely) expect to go back to an answer you have crossed off. Make sure to use your practice to improve your ability to eliminate more and more of the wrong answers with accuracy and pace.

You use time efficiently when you confirm right answers and eliminate wrong answers by comparing them against the passage and against the task in the question stem. You use time inefficiently when you compare answers against one another and think about which one is "more right." Hopefully, at the end of your first-round elimination process, there is an answer that stands out as being either certainly, or most likely, correct.

However, when there isn't an answer that looks great, or when there are two or more answers that seem correct, focus on trying to find what is right or wrong with these answers relative to text and task. Do not get stuck comparing the answers to one another, for you will surely get biased by their relative "attractiveness," and test writers are great at making right answers seem less attractive and wrong ones more so. Always keep your eye on the ball - work to match the text of one answer at a time against the passage and the question, and look for concrete reasons to like an answer or be suspicious of it.

Finally, you use time inefficiently when you get stuck on a question and spin your wheels. In general, the time that is most commonly wasted by all students is the time spent in indecision on questions that the student finds most difficult.

Essential Timing Habits

In just a few lessons, you will officially enter the final phase of your preparation (woo-hoo!). As we have discussed, the primary purpose of the final phase of your training is to develop the habits that will help you apply your skills at your best. When it comes to Reading Comprehension, there are three key habits I really want you to keep in mind.

One: Habitualized a Reading Pace

And make sure it's a brisk one. You want to read slowly enough that you can eventually understand why each part of the passage is there, but fast enough that you do not get bogged down in the details.

For most of us, the pressure of the exam (even the pressure of a timed practice test) wreaks havoc on our sense of time. We suddenly become terrible at estimating how long we are taking at reading a passage or answering a question. We can't help it—when we get to a certain point of focus or stress, our sense of time begins to wobble. That's why it's imperative that you habitualized a certain reading pace. Get used to reading all LSAT passages at a certain pace, and try to stay as consistent as possible throughout your practice while making your practice as realistic as possible. And get comfortable pushing that pace whenever you can.

Two: Go Fast on Questions That Go Fast

It's important to use perfect form, and it's important to get the questions we find easier right, but I also want to encourage you to push the pace during a question whenever you feel that your confidence is high and warranted. By this point, you know this test well, and there should be a lot of questions that go exactly as you expect—sometimes you can get through these questions in twenty seconds or less. Being able to go very fast on certain questions is a secret to the success of many top test takers—this leaves them plenty of time to carefully think through the situations that require more thought. Make sure you use your practice to work on getting through easier questions quickly while maintaining your accuracy.

<u>Three: Don't Spin Your Wheels</u>

If you were to take a sample section and time each question you solved, it is very likely that you'd discover at least four questions for which you spent two or more minutes. Of these four, it's very unlikely that you would get more than two correct—these questions take a long time because you don't understand them.

Those four problems likely took you about 8-9 minutes, which is 25% of the time you have for the section. Getting two correct answers in eight to nine minutes represents a terrible rate of return (if you were to extrapolate, it' be equivalent to getting 32 questions correct for the entire exam). You can get an advantage over most test takers if you can lessen the impact of these time-sucking questions - if you can develop a strong habit of spending no more than 1:30 on all but the most challenging questions, and no more than 2:00 on any one question, no matter how challenging that question is (that is, unless you have time to spare, as we'll discuss in just a bit.). Remember, harder questions aren't worth more points, and your goal is to answer and many questions right as possible. Invest your time in making sure you get right the ones you can, and make time for this by cutting your time on the toughest questions.

The Challenges of Reading Comprehension

In light of what we've just discussed, let's consider the general challenges that the Reading Comprehension section presents:

One: Passages can be dense and full of complex or subtle details.

Furthermore, the most difficult questions tend to be associated with those passages that have the most complex or nuanced content. Not only are these complex details necessary for answering certain questions, they impact our ability to read for reasoning structure. Most of us are not as good at using our reading ability when we are faced with unfamiliar subject matter.

Two: Central issues or passage structure can be complex or subtle.

When you think about a great piece of clothing, it can be great because of the materials (the substance of it) or the design (the use of that substance). Reading Comprehension passages can be difficult because of the content (the details involved) or because of the reasoning structure (the relationship between those details).

As you'll see with more experience, most reading passages will present two opposing viewpoints on some sort of issue (one opinion versus another on how a certain law should be interpreted, or an old scientific theory versus the one that replaced it). However, the relationship between these two sides is not always clear cut—in fact, it can be extremely subtle. Furthermore, most passages will inform us of the author's opinion of the content, but often this opinion will be given to us in vague ways, and the opinion can also be somewhat complex. Perhaps a passage will present two sides of an argument, and the author will hint that she somewhat agrees with one side, and feels uncertain about the other.

Thee: Questions require us to see the forest and the trees

That is, in order to answer questions successfully, we need to have a strong sense of the general structure of the passage, and, at the same time, we need to have a very clear sense of the details that are directly relevant to specific questions.

Many test takers end up trying to focus on both the big picture and the details as they read. In fact, most other preparation books, by giving you a laundry list of thirty specific and general things to notice as you read, indirectly point you toward just that tactic. But here's the thing—we can't do both well at the same time. Trying to see both the forest and the trees turns us into schizophrenic readers, and we end up doing both poorly. The key to success is to focus on the big picture as you initially read the passage, and to utilize specific details during the problem-solving process. We'll discuss this strategy quite a bit more in the lessons to come.

Timing Patterns for Top Scorers

When it comes to timing, top scorers in the Reading Comprehension section—those who are consistently able to miss two or fewer questions per section—typically share two common characteristics:

Top Scorers Have Time to Get through Every Step of the Process

In order to consistently answer questions correctly, we need to understand the reasoning structure of the passage, the task presented in the question stem, the reasons wrong answers are wrong, and the reason why the right answer is right—generally in that order. When you first started studying, you may have felt that it would be impossible to successfully satisfy these steps for each and every question; hopefully, you see more and more as you study that thinking about your process in terms of these steps not only makes you more accurate but faster, because it helps you use your time more efficiently.

When we are rushed for time, sometimes we need to move on from the passage to the questions without completely understanding the reasoning structure, and commonly we are forced to pick an answer without getting a chance to confirm with certainty that it is indeed correct or that the others are indeed incorrect. It is very hard to consistently score at a very high level if you are consistently facing these challenges. Top scorers are fast enough that their scores are not limited by these types of constraints.

They are fast enough to slow down when they need to as they read in order to understand reasoning structure, and they are fast enough to thoroughly vet the right answer, and every wrong answer, for almost all questions.

Top Scorers Can Finish the Section in Less Than Thirty-Five Minutes

Notice I said "can"—that doesn't mean a top scorer won't end up using all thirty-five minutes. The point I want to make is that top scorers are capable of going at a pace that would allow them to, if they choose not to spend a significant amount of extra time on any particular question, finish the section in well less than thirty-five minutes.

A typical Reading Comprehension section will have a few (anywhere from two to four, depending on the exam and how you tend to judge these things) questions that are extremely difficult to solve, even for top scorers. It's a huge advantage to have extra time for these questions. If, for example, you are able to consistently get through reading passages and answering all but the hardest two or three questions in a section in twenty-five minutes or less, then you know you have ten minutes or so for those two or three killer questions - in other words, as much time as you need. If your goal is to keep improving your score, and if you struggle at all with finishing in thirty-five minutes, your goal should be to limit the time you spend on the toughest questions. However, if you have improved to the point where you are trying to go -0 or -1 in a section, these toughest questions are your most important. Extra time for just these questions can be a huge advantage, and generally it's very hard to get a top score without it

Logical Reasoning: Sufficient Assumption & Supporting Principle

In this lesson, we are going to discuss two question types: Sufficient Assumption and Supporting Principle. For these two types of questions, what we want to do is figure out what is wrong, and then search for an answer to *completely fix* the issue. That's what Sufficient Assumption and Supporting Principle questions are asking us to do—find the answer that completely fixes the issues in the argument.

You'll note from the information on the side that these two question types are not that common. The reason we're covering just these two question types here is because we are also going to use this lesson to expand our discussion of conditional logic. In fact, we'll start with this. Most Sufficient Assumption questions involve conditional logic, and Sufficient Assumption questions most commonly present the most challenging conditional logic issues.

Conditional Logic 101

In this lesson, we introduced and discussed conditional reasoning in terms of four major Characteristics:

1. *Conditional Rules Are Rules That Only Apply Sometimes*

To be more specific, they are rules that are set off by a "trigger," more formally known as The sufficient condition. Why it is called the sufficient condition? Because it is sufficient, or enough, to guarantee the outcome. Speaking of which, the second characteristic we discussed was...

2. *Conditional Statements Represent Guarantees*
On the LSAT, "if " is a powerful and absolute word—it represents a guarantee. If the trigger takes effect or, more formally, if the sufficient condition is met, the outcome must result. This idea is fundamental to the make-up of the entire Logical Reasoning section.

It is the "guarantee" part of conditional statements that makes them so important to Logical Reasoning. One way to describe all flawed arguments is to say that they are arguments in which the author thinks the support is sufficient, or enough, when in fact it's not.

Notice how we fixed all of the flawed arguments from our "fill the hole" example—we needed to meld the support and premise with some sort of ironclad joint, and that's what a conditional statement provides. Notice that each correct response has a guarantee in it, and that guarantee can be thought of in terms of a trigger and a consequence.

3. *Conditional Statements Provide Inferences*
All conditional statements provide inferences known as contrapositives, and you can think of the original condition and the contrapositive as two different sides of the same coin. For challenging questions, the test writers will commonly give us our gap fillers in terms of their contrapositives. Consider these four answers we could have

gotten instead of the four answers we got above. Do you see that they give us the same information —the guarantee we needed?

4. *Conditional Statements Link Up*
Remember that there were certain games that had a lot of conditional rules, and when this was the case it was often necessary to link these conditions up in order to answer questions. There are certain Logical Reasoning questions that work this way as well. When you see multiple conditional statements in one stimulus, you know that a part of your job will be to see how these statements link up and how they don't.

Conditional Logic Language

What's mentioned on the left represents all of the major "rules" that you need to know for conditional logic, but that's not all that makes conditional logic on the Logical Reasoning section challenging. In fact, many people would argue that a bigger challenge is consistently interpreting conditional statements correctly.

There are various ways in which the test writers can write conditional relationships. Some of these ways make the relationship obvious, while others don't. In fact, there are certain conditional statements that force everyone, even those who have a wealth of formal logic experience, to stop and have to think carefully. In large part, this is because these conditional statements involve words to which, in real life, we give contextual (that is, not universal or absolute) meaning. "Only if " is a statement we use for different meanings in real life, and that's a big reason that it causes us so much trouble. Another word that similarly causes our brains to get fuzzy is the word "unless."

Let's break down the different ways in which conditional statements can be written, and work on developing a system for thinking about them whenever we are uncertain. We'll start by taking a close-up look at just one conditional statement.

Conditional-Heavy Stimuli

Just like certain games can be dominated by conditional rules, certain Logical Reasoning stimuli can be overrun by conditional logic statements. In most cases, just as in those types of games, the statements in these types of stimuli will link together.

This is only likely to happen in a few types of questions (Sufficient Assumption, Inference, Match the Flaw, and Match the Reasoning, most commonly) and will not happen more than once or twice per exam. However, these can often be some of the more intimidating questions in any Logical Reasoning section.

When you see a conditional-heavy stimulus for a Sufficient Assumption question ("What exactly is a Sufficient Assumption question?" you say! We'll get to that on the next page), what you can expect is that the supporting premises link together in some way to form the conclusion. Well actually, they almost link together. They are missing one link, and the correct answer will fill that link in.

Keep in mind that just because these stimuli have statements that link up does not mean you have to link them up. Oftentimes, hopefully most of the time, you will see the missing link without putting all the different pieces together. Other times you'll just simply see the missing link as a flaw in the argument, and not have to think about it in a conditional sense at all.

However, once in a while, there will be a question that will really require some strong linking skills. You want to be able to whip them out when you need them. You already have the ability to recognize and use the links from the Logic Games conditional logic lesson.

The extra challenge for Logical Reasoning problems, of course, is that you also need to translate these statements and strip them down before you link them.
Below are examples of a more obvious missing link, and a better hidden one. You want to avoid doing the heavy work when you can, but you also want to make sure you feel you can do it when you need to.

Passage Topics

The LSAT doesn't want to favor anyone with a specific undergraduate degree, so it provides a mix of topics.

1. <u>Science</u>
These passages deal with such topics as chemistry

and astronomy and a raging debate relating to a certain scientific issue. Note that science issues often involve cause-and-effect relationships (and the essay questions will revolve around this purported relationship).

Science is often subjective. We tend to think of scientific facts as being static and of the scientists themselves as clear and logical, like Spock on Star Trek. In reality, science is full of controversy and conflicting ideas. Science essays on the LSAT will often foray into controversy and it's your job as the reader to see the different points of view, biases, and the conflict.

2. Law

These essays may also be jargon intensive. While you may already have some background knowledge – it is usually beneficial if you do as it makes the passage easier to read – just remember that specific, outside knowledge will never be strictly necessary to answer an essay question. All the answers you need can be found in the essay itself.

3. Cultural Studies

A large number of these essays focus on historically oppressed groups (their art, culture, and history). The passage's tone will generally be sympathetic.

4. Society

These essays will discuss public policy-related issues. Any viewpoint won't be terribly radical. It will adopt a tone and style that you would expect in a typical American law school.

Passage Structure

Opinion
The author has an opinion and this is expressed in the essay. Often the author advocates a particular position, often against another point of view. Think of this author as an idea salesman who wants you to become a True Believer and reject opposing opinions.

Debate
These essays have two different points of view that often clash in a debate-style. The two points of view are argued forcefully. This is common with the dual-passage format (which features two passages instead of a longer one). You need to grasp the two opposing points of view and the areas of disagreement.

Synthesis
In this type of essay, there are generally two different points of view that spawn a third one, which combines elements of the original two.

Presentation Styles

Case Study
These passages will revolve around an event or an example or something happening, with a discussion of what it means or what can be discerned from it.

Cause and Effect
In the passages you'll see a structure revolving around something causing something else and explanations for this causal relationship. Cause and

Effect is a major topic in the Logical Reasoning section, as well. It's covered in this section.

Similarly, you will find questions often related to Cause and Effect on the Reading Comprehension, such as Strengthening and Weakening. Reading Comprehension is mostly just Logical Reasoning with a longer attention span.

Inquiry/Explanation

A riddle wrapped in a mystery inside an enigma — These questions will pose a question (a paradox or unexplained phenomenon) and then present possible answers/explanations. The controversy in the passage will revolve around the explanation (and so will the questions). The main point will be easy to spot: It's the answer to the question.

Categories

These passages will revolve around the classification of something. Either it can be classified in one category, or another.

How to solve this section:

The section consists of long passages which you need to read as quickly as possible. You should be prepared for active Reading as you identify the vital points.

Tactics to cope well with Reading and analyzing Top LSAT Classes teach comprehension passages. After identifying and understanding the points posited by the author, the next step is to begin answering the questions. The scope of the question asked is quite limited, and top LSAT courses will take you through these important types of questions to assist you in identifying what is being asked and rightly apply it to the passage.

Once that has been sorted, you will not have a hard time choosing the right answer from the multiple choice questions.

Writing Sample

The last section of the LSAT is the writing sample section. It starts with an argument with some information about a step that needs to be taken. You will be given two choices and some criteria to inform your decision. You are expected to state what informs your choice based on presented facts; you could also cite any external knowledge or personal reasoning. It's important to note that the writing sample will not add to your score. Instead, your hand-written essay is useful for reference purpose in your LSAC law school report, which could be accessed by law schools you apply to for admission.

Some law schools take a particular interest in applicants writing samples, and it can decide the fate of two applicants if one applicant doesn't perform well. This means you shouldn't take it with levity even if it is not added to your score.

Several law schools will view your writing samples, and you may want to know precisely what they will be looking forward to seeing. This study guide will give you valuable assistance as you formulate an impressive writing sample.

The LSAT Writing Sample asks you to write an essay in 35 minutes. It is wise to invest a few hours in preparation for your essay. Those who don't prepare at all often write terrible essays. These essays might even be bad enough to endanger a student's admission chances. Spend a few hours looking at sample essays to avoid any unnecessary mistakes.

The essay section is designed to test how well you can (1) organize a compelling argument using sound reasoning and supporting evidence and (2) express your thoughts clearly in written form. The essay section is NOT meant to test how many big vocabulary words you know, how much you know about the law or any other specific topic, or really even how creative you are.

What Will the Topic Be?

You won't be asked to write about a specific topic so much as you'll be asked to respond to a specific scenario. The scenario will always be presented in the same form. Here's a watered-down example (keep in mind that the scenario on your exam will be more involved):

John wants to buy a pet. He is choosing between a cat and a dog. He only has time to care for one pet. Write an essay in which you argue for the purchase of one type of pet over the other based on the following considerations:

John wants a pet that will be relatively maintenance-free.
John wants a pet that will be a true, loyal companion.

The first option, the cat, is a clean pet that does not typically damage or destroy household property.

While the cat does need to be fed twice per day, it does not need to be taken for daily walks. The cat is very aloof and non-responsive to human interaction, but it does grow attached to its human owner over time.

The second option, the dog, requires daily attention. The dog has been known to damage household property, and it requires walks on a daily basis. With training, the dog can learn to be relatively self-sufficient. The dog responds to human interaction and craves the attention of its human owner, but it can't communicate very well with humans.

As mentioned earlier, the scenario will always be presented in the same way. The first part will present a choice, the second part (the bullet statements) will present two considerations that need to be weighed in making that choice, and the third part will provide more information about the two choices at hand. Notice that there is no right or wrong answer here. In fact, the scenario is presented in such a way as to make it difficult to decide which option is better! They both have their pros and cons. What's important is NOT which option you choose, but rather how you justify, or support, the choice that you do end up making.

How Should I Write My Essay?

The following will outline a process for planning and writing your essay. It certainly isn't the only way to do it, but it does provide a consistent, repeatable approach that you'll be able to rely on.

Step 1: Compile information in grid form (5 minutes total for steps 1-3)

In the test booklet, set up a table that has the two choices along the top and the two considerations along the side. In the intersecting cells of the grid, include the appropriate pros and cons using a "+" before any pro and a "-" before any con. For our example, it might look like this:

Cat	Dog
Relatively Maintenance Free	-Needs Food Twice a Day
+Doesn't Destroy Property	-Damages Property
+No Walks	-Daily Attention
+Can Learn to be Fairly Self-Sufficient	-Daily Walks
-Can't Communicate Well	+Becomes Attached to Human Owner
-Aloof and Non-Responsive	+Craves Human Attention
	+Responds to Humans
	+ True and Loyal Companion

You're familiar with cats and dogs, so it's probably already obvious to you that a cat would be a good low-maintenance choice and a dog would be good for companionship. Keep in mind, however, that the scenario you will see on your exam will be much less familiar to you. Organizing the information in grid form will make it much easier for you to see the relative strengths and weaknesses of each choice.

Step 2: Decide on a "more important" consideration (5 minutes total for steps 1-3)

At this point, you want to make a decision. Is it more important for John that the pet be maintenance-free or that it be a loyal companion? Again, there's no right answer. Even so, you need to decide which you will make more important. Choose one that you can easily justify (even if it's a made-up justification). For example, we'll decide:

"Having a loyal companion is more important than having a low-maintenance pet because true friendship trumps all else. If John has a true companion and friend, the daily maintenance will become a labor of love instead of a hassle."

Step 3: Make your choice! (5 minutes total for steps 1-3)

Your decision in step 2 should lead you to a clear choice. In this case, if we deem companionship to be the more important consideration, then we'll want to choose the dog (since the dog clearly has more compelling plusses in that part of the grid).

"John should pick the dog because it will serve as a more loyal companion than the cat will."

Step 4: Write an essay (25 minutes)

Plan on structuring your essay the same way every time. Here's an easy template to follow:

Essay Section Template

Paragraph 1:

A. Summarize the decision to be made. "The scenario presented above puts John in a position in which he will choose between purchasing a cat and purchasing a dog."

B. Acknowledge the complexity of the decision. "Given the considerations and characteristics of the choices at hand, this is a very difficult decision in that each choice has its merits."

C. State your opinion. "Even so, John would be better served by choosing the dog."

Paragraph 2:

A. State why the primary consideration (the one you chose to be the primary consideration) is more important and how your choice satisfies this consideration. "First, it is more important to have a pet that serves as a loyal companion than it is to have a pet that is maintenance-free..." (justify this statement, even if it's a made-up justification) or "The dog will be a loyal companion in that it will ..." (use the information from the grid to show how)

B. State why the other choice (cat) falls short in this regard. "The cat, on the other hand, is a poor match for anyone looking for a loyal pet ..." (use the information from the grid to show how)

Paragraph 3:

State how your choice still does an okay job with the secondary consideration. “Furthermore, while the dog isn’t an ideal choice for someone wanting a maintenance-free pet, it can learn to be relatively self-sufficient…” (use any other information from the grid to support this)

Paragraph 4:

Summarize your argument

Step 5: Proofread! (5 minutes)

Spelling errors, misprints, grammatical errors, etc. will never go over well. While a few simple mistakes won’t kill you, you want to be sure your final essay is as clean as possible.

Practice this a few times on some real essay prompts and you should be all set. Good luck!

Analytical Reasoning

Steps to prepare adequately for LSAT Analytical Reasoning test

To have a high score in analytical reasoning, you should be able to:

- Solve a problem making use of the information given.
- Know how to solve the problem with your knowledge of “if-then” scenario.

- Identify true or false statements based on information at your disposal.
- Use existing information to draw inferences.
- Recognize logically equivalent statements.

While you don't need specialized logic training, you are expected to understand how to point out specific associations within the text and apply them meaningfully to the questions. It is imperative to stick to the information given in the passage or related to it. Introducing information gotten from others or stating your personal opinions can impact negatively on the answers given.

The ideal way to answer questions bordering on analytical reasoning is to create a visual representation of indicated "rules" in the passage. This will serve as a reference to getting the right answers.

This test requires you to choose whether a statement must, or could, be true, based on a given set of information or facts. The used passages will be centered on an event with a form of order or sequence. Practicing analytical reasoning will significantly improve your likelihood of scoring well in this section of the LSAT. As you study, ensure you consider the following.

Terms to Know

Having a good grasp of specific terms will benefit you in the process of reading and answering questions. Ensure you thoroughly understand the meaning and how it's used.

<u>If-Then Statements</u>

For statements related to the “If-then” situation, you are expected to draw logical conclusions and inferences, centered on the information available. You can also refer to an if-then statement as a conditional statement; with the “then” representing the conclusion which depends solely on the variable “if.” For instance, you could see a conditional statement such as, “If you work hard, you will go far.” The word go far depends on hard work.

You may also encounter some inaccurate if-then statements which you may need to identify as such. These are referred to as fallacies. An illustration of an inaccurate uncertain statement is, “If you abide by the law, you will wind up in a courtroom.” Being law abiding should Following the law should prevent a crime-free life and not otherwise.

Logical Equivalence

This refers to the way in which one describes the equivalent logic of two dissimilar statements. An ideal example can be found in pairs of words like A - If Jane is registered in school, she is given homework regularly. B - If Jane is not enrolled in school, she doesn’t get homework to do.

Even though these are two different sentences, they have the same logical conclusions. Note that most logical equivalences won’t be as simple as the example above, but applying your basic knowledge about logical arguments will help you identify whether they are equivalent or different.

Specific Skills to Practice

It’s necessary to be well-skilled in reasoning and practice these entire before the test day.

Making Inferences

You need to reach a logical conclusion from the clues and leading information given in the text. In a story, it could mean concluding regards to each characters nature. Within the law, it implies drawing a conclusion with the use of case history or concluding a law from its context and the tone.

When making an inference, go through all material given as a reference and the circumstances that surround the conclusion you intend to draw. This could also imply that you get prepared for logical guesswork and concluding even with concrete facts or evidence missing.

Revising Based on New Information

There is a constant change in law-based work, which means you should be open to adapting and shifting your understanding as more information is unraveled. Although you may be tempted to be a little bit rigid about your opinion as it appears as the only possibility, understand that it's not the nature of law. As new information gets to you, thoroughly peruse every detail, and process this information along with current information to reach an all-inclusive, evidence-based conclusion.

Comprehension

As you strive to comprehend every piece of information at your disposal, ensure you thoroughly read each of them. Next step is to find where there are similarities or information widely applicable to merge cases or problems. On a final note, work to proffer solution to the issues at hand, such as the way to present a case, how to portray a series of relationships, how a shift is scheduled and modify employee interaction, etc. Be prepared to make further findings and research if you don't understand some things; take up every opportunity to learn as it will be helpful for the future.

Tips and Tricks

Below are a few ideas needed to make an effective test-taking experience.

Read Carefully

There are several keywords and essential phrases littered around this test questions and passages, do well to identify them as you read through. The meaning of sentences, even seemingly straightforward ones are altered through can be altered with a change in the word.

Jot down some salient words and phrases as you read on so you can refer to it later.

Independence of Questions

All questions standalone and are not in any way connected in this test. While one may wish you draw parallels and form interdependence, you are meant to view each question and evaluate them in isolation, instead of in a group or series.

Use Tools

In the course of reading and solving the questions, don't hesitate to seek external assistance. This could be in the aspect of diagrams, notes, highlighted words, etc. Although fewer amounts of time should be spent on these but they can prove useful while combining the information given and making inferences.

Logical Reasoning

General Information

This Logical Reasoning section comprises of two parts with each contributing 50 percent to the total possible points. A short passage will be given, which you are to read and answer the corresponding questions.

This section aims to ascertain your skills in critical thinking and access your ability to take part in an argument objectively.

For instance, you may be tasked with the responsibility of faulting the author's line of thought reasoning or decide on what fact would significantly weaken the author's argument. Usually, your test will center around this theme namely: argument or conclusion, strengthening/weakening, argument or reasoning method; questions which border on principle; inference; identify the issue; key point; must be true; parallel reasoning; and paradox.

While attempting these questions, ensure you don't include your personal previous experience or knowledge on the subject matter.

Also, ensure your answers are in tandem with the question asked and not just a true statement. Some questions may have lots of parts associated with it, and you will need to ensure your answer satisfies all.

Terms to Know

Get acquainted with these terms and their meanings. Also, understand how they are used when answering questions.

Argument

An argument can be defined as a set of statements made to support or prove a conclusion. An argument has at least one or several premises while it leads to a single conclusion. For instance:

All mangoes are fruits.

No fruits are square.

Therefore, no mangoes are square.

This is another example of a formal logic argument, or syllogism. You can find it in the form: *All A are B, No B are C. Thus, no A are C.*These are deductive arguments, which are always valid. When you are studying, be sure to pay attention not only to the parts of the argument, but also to their forms.

Premise

The places of an argument are statements that assume the conclusion is true. It's purpose is to prove the conclusion directly or by inference. For example:

The concert would be ruined if Christina Aguilera lost her voice,

Christina Aguilera lost her voice.

Therefore, the concert was ruined.

This is generally in the form: *All A are F. X is F. Therefore X is A.* This is inconsistent because even if both premises are true, the conclusion can still be false. Right? What if she had a smash warm-up act?

Assumption

An assumption is a statement in which there was no proof offered. It is intended to be taken as true. It is the bridge between the premise and the conclusion. In other words, arguments rely on assumptions. No evidence is offered for the premises set forth themselves to prove the conclusion. They are *assumed* to be true. For example, here is a classic syllogism:

All men are mortal.;

Socrates is a man.;

Therefore, Socrates is mortal.

Here, the first two statements, the premises, are *assumed* to be true by the author. So, as you can see, every argument always includes assumptions.

Conclusion

The conclusion is the statement in the argument, the truth of which is intended to be proven by the argument. Using our earlier syllogism, developed by Aristotle:

All men are mortal.

Socrates is a man.

Therefore, Socrates is mortal.

This is the conclusion. It is what the author is trying to prove or convince others to believe or think. Based on the premises and inferences that could be drawn from them, Aristotle intended to show that Socrates was mortal. Each argument contains *one* conclusion. Sometimes, they begin with words such as *therefore*, *wherefore*, *in conclusion*, etc.

Specific Skills to Practice

The Logical Reasoning section of the LSAT is another way to test your critical thinking ability. Practice using these skills.

Identifying Parts of an Argument and How They Relate to One Another

As we've mentioned, there are several parts to any argument: the premise(s), assumption, and conclusion. We have not yet discussed *inference*. An inference is where a new understanding or belief stems from the first belief or proposition. Inference also draws us from proposition or premise to conclusion. *Inferring* is drawing conclusions from premises. There are *deductive* and *inductive* inferences, the former nearly guaranteeing the validity of its conclusion, while the latter saying entirely that it is probable. Understand that *assumption* is different from *inference*. *Assumptions* are statements in which there was no proof offered, while *inferences* are new beliefs formed from premises.

Assumption and inference are both similar in a way that they can lead to the conclusion, but are different in their operation. Both may be needed in an argument to reach a logical conclusion. For example:

A mango is a fruit.

John likes fruit.

Therefore, John likes mangoes.

Without reaching into the validity of the argument, see that the first premise is also an *assumption*, as it is taken as true that a mango is a fruit. The same with the second premise. From those premises we *infer* that John likes mangoes. We form a new belief. This is different from assumption, although as you can see, both are necessary in the argument.

Identifying Similarities and Differences between Reasoning Patterns

For the LSAT, you will be asked to choose the answer that most conforms to the argument pattern of the passage or "stimulus." It's called *parallel reasoning*. This is when having even a rudimentary understanding of argument forms can help a lot. These questions can take more time than most to answer because of the extra text and the time it takes to do the comparisons. Diagramming in the margins can always help speed things up and help you keep the questions clear in your head. For example:

Argument: *All penguins have wings and all birds have wings, therefore they are alike.* Choose:

(a) *Birds and penguins are alike; however, they have a lot of dissimilarities.*

(b) *All birds have wings. Penguins are just like birds, therefore they must have wings.*

(c) *Shrimp and fish must be alike because every fish has eyes and so does every shrimp.*

(d) *All rats have tails and all monkeys have tails.*

(e) *Some snakes are cold-blooded and almost all reptiles are cold-blooded, therefore, snakes are reptiles.*

The secret when choosing for the right answer is to forget about all of the descriptive words, birds, snakes, etc. and make sure to only consider how the original argument is structured. Then find an answer with the same structure. Diagramming the structure of the argument could look like this:

All of A have Q.

All of B have Q.

Therefore, A and B are alike.

Which answer choice fits this pattern?

It is (c).

Every fish (A) has eyes (Q).

Every shrimp (B) has eyes (Q).

Therefore, A and B must be alike.

The arrangement of the argument has been changed, but you can see when you diagram it that it has the same elements.

Developing Well-Supported Conclusions

A substantial conclusion will have premises that are plainly true, or at least easily accepted as true, and the conclusion will clearly follow, or be easily inferred, from the premises. If your premises are weak or if it's not convincing, your argument will likely fail. By the same token, if the conclusion cannot be concluded from the premises, that conclusion will also likely fail. Even so, some might still believe the conclusion, if it is true, but you will have greatly lessened your chances of convincing others of the validity of your argument. For example:

Mangoes are fruit.

All fruits rot.

Therefore, mangoes rot.

The premises are easy to accept and the conclusion abide logically from them. Consider:

Mangoes are fruit.

All fruits taste good.

Therefore, mangoes taste good.

This argument has less teeth. The first premise can easily be accepted as true, but the second may be considered as false by others. The conclusion then may also be considered as false.

Using Analogy in Reasoning

When you *insist by analogy*, you show that at least two things (ideas, things, people) are similar in one or more ways and that because of that they must also be similar in another way. For example:

Mangoes and Papayas are tropical fruits that taste good.

Mangoes are good for you.

Papayas are good for you.

The form of these arguments is generally:

1-4* all have properties A and B.

1-3 have property C also.

Thus, 4 probably also has property C.

*(for illustration purposes)

This is exactly what we've done in our example.

Mangoes (1) and Papayas (2) are tropical fruits (A) that taste good (B).

Mangoes (1) are good for you (C).

(Therefore) Papayas are good for you (C).

There are several things to keep in mind when making and analyzing *analogical arguments.* The more *cases* of similarity that you have, the stronger your argument. In other words, if we had three or four fruits that tasted good and were good for you instead of just one, that would be better. The similarities must always be *relevant* to the conclusion. Also, you want as few *differences* as possible because they weaken your conclusion. Lastly, and this is by no means the last factor affecting analogical arguments, *diversity* of cases of similarity. The more different cases you have with the relevant similarities, the stronger your conclusion. So if five different people all saw the same movie at different times, in different theatres, some in IMAX , 3D, and 2D and all gave it five stars, that is diversity.

Identifying Areas of Disagreement or Misunderstandings in an Argument

Commonly called as "point at issue," this question will ask you to look or identify the point of disagreement between two speakers in a passage. The most important thing to remember is that it is unlikely to be their conclusions, but rather premises, inferences, or assumptions. Analyze the arguments and find where the disagreement lies, without supplying any additional information yourself, and you will have your answer. For example:

Gregory: Texting while driving is too common among teenage girls than any male age group. Recent accident data have confirmed this. Cell phones should be banned.

Olivia: Texting while driving is a danger to us all. However, cell phones serve a legitimate purpose otherwise. Cars must be equipped with cell reception blocking technology to prevent the use of cell phones while driving.

So, what do they disagree on? They *agree* that texting while driving is bad. They *agree* that something has to be done about it. They *disagree* that cell phones must be banned, or put another way, they *disagree* that cell phones should be allowed to remain among the populace. Be assured that the questions on the LSAT will not be so simplistic. However, if you stay within the argument and search for the parts that overlap, you should be able to tell the agreements from the disagreements.

Explaining the Effect(s) of Additional Evidence on an Argument

As mentioned earlier, you can have deductive or inductive arguments supporting your conclusion. In the case of an *inductive* argument, where you have not insured your result, but merely inferred that it is probable, additional evidence could very well tip the scales in either direction. In fact, one way to know if an argument is, in fact, inductive is to consider whether additional evidence would make a difference. In the case of a valid *deductive* argument, if its premises are true, if the conclusion is established on the premises, it *has to* be true. Therefore, additional evidence will not alter the conclusion. You will be asked questions about whether certain "evidence" will strengthen or weaken an argument. You might first try to evaluate whether it is an inductive or valid deductive argument as we have just discussed. Additional evidence leading towards the argument's assumption(s) can also strengthen or weaken it dramatically.

Identifying Assumptions Used in Presenting an Argument.

In many arguments, the underlying assumption (See: *Assumption*, above) will not be *explicit*, or stated, but *implicit*, or hidden. Knowing how to spot these assumptions can be the key to finding the issue(s) in an argument. For example:

Abortion is wrong because it is killing.

The implied or implicit assumption is *All killing is wrong*. The argument is invalid without this assumption. It doesn't mean that this is the end of the argument, but it is just a statement on form. Finding these assumptions requires first finding the premises and conclusion. As we've discussed, the assumption is the link between them. Some words that represent premises may be *because*, *since*, *as*, *in view of*, and so forth. Words that represent a conclusion may be *accordingly*, *clearly*, *hence*, *so*, *thus*, and so on. When you have determined the premises and conclusion, determine if the argument is valid. (See: *Argument* above, generally.) If that is the case, the assumption will have been shown explicitly from the premises and the conclusion follows therefrom. If it is not valid, what premises are required to make it so? These are the *implicit* or hidden assumptions.

Finding and Using Principles and Rules in an Argument

Some would insist the difference between principles and rules in philosophy and law. Principles are standards that can be satisfied based on legal and factual possibility. They are what we use to identify which rule to apply. Rules are norms or standards that either do or do not apply and will or will not be implemented. Black and white. However, the rules of logic, and therefore critical thinking, are a bit distinct. For example:

If A then B

A

Therefore B

This is another form that is called "modus ponens." If you find an argument in this form, it will be a valid argument in that its conclusion follows from its assumption(s). So basically if the assumption(s) are true, the conclusion *must* also be true. There are several valid forms that you need to know, including "modus tollens," "disjunctive syllogism," "hypothetical syllogism," "constructive dilemma," and "destructive dilemma." Knowing these forms will help you recognize a valid argument and apply your analysis of the truth or falsity of the assumptions to identify or for you to know the truth of the conclusion. (We will discuss fallacies below.)

Finding and Explaining Flaws in an Argument

Mistakes in arguments, or errors in reasoning, are called “logical fallacies.” There are a number of logical fallacies one can fall prey to in an argument. You would do well to know at least the most common of them. For example: “Begging the Question.” This is also known as the “circular argument” because the premises tried to prove the conclusion with the conclusion itself. In other words, the conclusion is embedded within the premises as a way to get the same conclusion. For example:

Violent video games don’t hurt children because children are no more violent or agitated after playing them.

Another common fallacy is the “Slippery Slope” where the author begins with a proposition then follows it with a progression of unsupported propositions to an “inevitable” conclusion. For example:

Women shouldn’t eat grapes. If they eat grapes, they will eat M&M’s. Then they will gain forty pounds and their husbands will suddenly leave them. Then they will fall short on the mortgage and lose their homes. Women cannot eat grapes or we will have an increased population of homeless.

You see why it is called a slippery slope? There will be times that the offending premise(s) is implied. You will then have to rely on your skills at pulling out the implied premise, then spotting the fallacy. This is where knowing your valid forms helps, as well.

Finding Explanations in an Argument

First, it is important to understand that explanations and arguments, though quite similar and easily merged, are not the same. Often times, it can be difficult to tell them apart. An explanation consists of two parts: the thing, event, phenomenon to be explained, *explanandum*, and the part that does the explaining, *explanans*. Another way to spot an explanation is to see if any new knowledge is offered such that one could learn from it, rather than evidence to convince you of the truth of a conclusion. Because both argument and explanation are forms of reasoning, it can be easy to get them confused. For example:

My brother is sick.

If this is going to be an argument, it would go on to offer *grounds*, *reasons*, or *evidence* to answer the question "How do you know?"

Because my brother has a fever of 102, my brother is sick.

This is an argument because it provides evidence to support the conclusion that "my brother is sick." Sounds like a definition though, doesn't it? Don't forget those implied premises.

My brother has a fever of 102.

All persons with fevers of 102 are sick.

Therefore my brother is sick.

If the statement were to be made into a definition, it would offer a cause to answer the question "Why?"

My brother is sick with a fever of 102 caused by his body raising its own temperature to fight off invading bacteria.

In this case, you were granted with new facts so that you would learn from them, not to prove that "my brother is sick."

Reading Comprehension

This test will evaluate your ability to read and understand written material and is similar to other reading comprehension tests in this way. However, on the LSAT, the reading comprehension section is different in these important ways:

- You have to be able to read very precisely and ferret out very specific details.
- Reading passages are dense and complex.
- Content is of the same level that you will encounter in law school.
- The passage writers apply high-level vocabulary and complicated rhetorical structure.

This section of the LSAT contains four sets of passages and questions. Three of the sets consists one passage, followed by five to eight questions. The fourth set consists of two passages, followed by questions. In this fourth set, the questions will ask you to compare and contrast information given in the two passages.

LSAT reading passages are drawn from multiple disciplines, including the social sciences, biological and physical sciences, the humanities, and concepts of law. The text will include complicated vocabulary and argument structure. There may be multiple viewpoints presented in a very sophisticated manner.

The questions you will face involves using the passage to:

- Identify the author's purpose or the main idea.
- Locate facts that are explicitly stated.
- Make inferences from the text.
- Identify words as they are used in a passage.
- Tell how the passage is organized.
- Discover information that can be applied in a new situation or context.
- Identify functional principles that apply to the passage.
- Develop analogies for information given in the passage.
- Make judgments about the attitude of the author based on his/her tone.
- Provide new information that would impact the author's claims.

Concepts to Understand

Main Idea or Primary Purpose

The main idea (or primary purpose) of a piece is the central idea around which the work is organized. In a compelling essay, for instance, the main idea (also called a thesis) might be that cats make better pets than ferrets. In a narrative, the main idea is likely to be more nuanced, and may be the growth of a character, or the unraveling of a community.

Explicitly Stated Information

Explicitly specified information is information precisely addressed in a text. If something is stated explicitly, it is not utilizing figurative language and is not meant to be inferred. It is guiding the audience directly to an idea or information.

Ideas that can be Inferred

The opposite of direct stated information is inferred information. While direct stated information may be found directly in the text, inferences must be reached by the audience. When inferring information, look at the information surrounding the text. Relationships, occurrences, or even supporting details may be involved. Sometimes, in the sentence, “Rose decided not to go to the party, as she had nothing to wear,” it is clearly stated that Rose both has decided against attending a party and that she has nothing to wear. It is concluded that Rose does not, in fact, have an absolute shortage of clothing, but that she feels she does not have to wear party-appropriate attire.

Organization or Structure of a Passage

The organization or structure of a passage is the direction in which ideas are presented. In a basic essay, the most common method of organization is the five-paragraph structure: introduction, body, and conclusion. There will be one paragraph each for the introduction and the conclusion and three paragraphs for the body.

But this structure is not the only way to arrange a piece—particularly in fiction. Fiction often uses flashbacks to tell a story, making the piece more erratic in structure rather than strictly linear. Some essays might show the conclusion first, then provide supporting details.

Organization is significant for two reasons: It provides clarity for the author and reader. A well-organized story or essay guides the reader along, rather than making them guess at what is being said or where the piece is going. Simultaneously, it provides a rhythmic structure for the writer to follow. The manner in which a piece is organized can provide insight into the intentions of an author, and the goal of a particular passage. For instance, an author who uses flashbacks may wish to acquaint the reader with a situation as it is, then gradually explain the reason for the occurrence. In a passage, the structure typically shows which information is considered the most important or the most pertinent.

Specific Skills to Practice

Apply Information to New Context

The context of a word, passage, or idea is crucial because it provides insight into the meaning of that word, passage, or idea. It is not enough to only be able to divide the meaning of something in its original context, however; you must be able to take the information provided and understand it and apply it to a new context. Sometimes, if you and your friend are talking about fish in an aquarium, and he/she utters the phrase, “Don’t get too close to the edge,” your friend is likely talking about keeping away from the edge of an aquarium. If that phrase is uttered in an undercover investigation, however, the meaning changes based upon the context—you have to be able to discern the difference in meaning in the same phrase in different surroundings.

Determine Word/Phrase Meaning from Context

Determining the meaning of a word or phrase from the context involves looking at the word (or phrase) in question and searching the surrounding area for clues as to what it means. For instance, look at the following sentence:

"Andrew was unscrupulous in many of his dealings, leading to the majority of his clients leaving for more principled partners."

For this sentence, what does the word *unscrupulous* mean? Given that Andrew's clients are leaving for principled partners, it is safe to assume that the meaning is not a pleasing one. From there, you can look at the word *principled*, and its use as an antonym to *unscrupulous*. It is then safe to assume that the meaning is anything along the lines of *unprincipled* or *questionable*.

Identify Principles Used in the Passage

To know the principles used in a passage, first read the passage through. From there, go back through, focusing on the most pertinent information offered. What are the supporting details? What is given greater weight within the text? Answering these questions will describe key principles—even somewhat obscured ones.

Form Analogies for Arguments in the Passage

To form analogies for arguments, you have to first identify what exactly the argument is in a favor of, or against. When you have a clear idea what the argument is, look for a similar argument. Sometimes, if an argument in a paper is arguing for the use of euthanasia chambers in animal shelters, but speaking out against the lack of animal cruelty laws in the area, you might form an analogy such as, "Arguing for euthanasia while gunning for stricter animal cruelty laws is like supporting gun control, but encouraging more men and women to purchase firearms: it doesn't quite make sense."

Identify the Author's Attitude from Tone and/or Language

Author's attitude can be tricky. However, with a little help from the language used in a piece and the overall tone of a piece, the task is manageable. First, a look at the tone. Is the tone of a piece serious? Lighthearted? Angry? Confrontational? Read the work, and identify what type of feeling or "vibe" you get from the overall piece. From there, analyze word usage. Are words large and nearly indecipherable? The author might be working to plea as an authority on the manner. Is the language sarcastic and biting? The author might be demonstrating derision for the subject.

Analyze the Effect of New Information on the Passage Disagreement

To analyze the effect of new information of the passage argument, first identify the strength and motive of the argument. From there, connect the new information and re-examine the main idea and supporting details of the argument. Are they weakened? Does the point hit home even harder? Is the argument belittled? The most effective means of determining this is to identify the argument, add in the new information, and go over or reread the passage. This will illustrate any faults, flaws, weaknesses, or strengths that are more apparent than before.

Compare Two Passages

When comparing two passages, focus on the resemblance; to do the opposite is to contrast. Read one passage, identify its purpose and meaning, and move on to the next. As you read, search for similarities between the two. There may be resemblance in tone, writing style, language, or purpose—the possibility for similarity is nearly endless. As you analyze, be thorough and identify first any resemblance or similarity in subject. From there, look for similarities in wording and style. Next, look for similar tones. Continue exhausting each of these avenues until you have determined the parallels in the passages.

Tips and Tricks

Identify Your Own Strategy

To determine your own test-taking strategy, plan ahead and practice. First, try reading the passage, then analyzing the questions. Next, try reading the passage and then reading the questions. While there is no right answer, it can make a significant difference both in time and in energy when you know how you are best able to perceive information.

Mark Helpful Words and Points as You Read

Rather than blasting through a passage and looking for important information later, make a note of anything you think might be important, interesting, or helpful. While not all of these notes may be helpful or would come in handy, you will drastically cut down your testing time by being prepared.

Base Your Answer Only on Material Presented

Although it can be difficult to overcome bias, it is very important to focus on the passage at hand, regardless of any prior knowledge you might have, or your own opinion on the subject. If a passage contains information regarding a conspiracy you find ludicrous, for instance, curb your own opinion and search the passage for facts and information pertinent to the questions at hand. The test is not there to measure your opinion, or even test your knowledge, but your ability to clearly and concisely follow directions.

Compare Two Passages Carefully

Be meticulous in your comparisons. Do not simply recognize or identify similar ideas in a passage, but similar word choice, backgrounds, author attitude, and more. Comparison requires a comprehensive reading of both passages, as well as a basic understanding of the conventions of English. As you prepare for the exam, exercise on comparing two passages—even ones that are seemingly polar opposites. This will give you confidence and the skill needed to adequately compare.

Some of the Most Challenging Passages Used in Previous Tests - Look Them Up and Use Them When Studying

Students wanting to test themselves against the toughest Reading Comprehension passages often ask us where they can find the hardest passages that have ever appeared in the RC section. Below is a list of the 10 hardest LSAT Reading Comprehension passages of all time, accompanied by our at-times jesting commentary. The list is presented in chronological order:

1. **October 1991, Passage #3: Waterbugs**
   This was the first "hard science" passage ever to appear on the LSAT. The passage discusses adaptive responses in organisms, and features an extended discussion of developmental responses in waterbugs (hence the passage name). The text included such fun terms as "dimorphic," "macropterous," and "micropterous," which were quickly forgotten by most students once the passage ended.
2. **February 1994, Passage #4: Civil Rights Theories**
   This passage contained only six questions, but the discussion of classical social psychological theories ("relative deprivation" and "J-curve," to name two) in

Civil Rights movement literature caused fits for most students.

3. **December 1995, Passage #2: Hard Cases and Texture**
   This is one of several passages to include the views of Ronald Dworkin, a noted legal scholar. Regrettably, the topic under discussion—about legal cases that contain highly controversial issues that are not easily resolved—ventures into a nearly impenetrable discussion of legal principles.
4. **December 1998, Passage #2: Personal Names**
   This may be the most difficult passage on this list. The passage discusses personal names, and references John Stuart Mills, Claude Levi-Strauss, and the Hopis of the southwestern U.S. A passage about people's names sounds fun, but this one wasn't.
5. **June 1999, Passage #3: Steady-state Economics**
   Steady-state economics is a new school of economics, one that most people didn't want to learn more about after reading this passage. The text at times delves into deep economic theory and then, to make matters worse, the passage contains eight questions.
6. **6. October 2000, Passage #2: Multicultural Education**
   This is possibly the easiest of

the ten passages on the list. Of course, because this list is about the ten hardest LSAT passages of all time, that still makes this passage extremely challenging. Here's a brief, fair-use sample of the text: "The Western scientific heritage is founded upon an epistemological system that prizes the objective over the subjective, the logical over the intuitive and the empirically verifiable over the mystical." Umm, yeah, what he said.

7. **December 2005, Passage #4: Embryo Polarity**
   Overall, this was a difficult RC section because the second passage—about Louise Gluck—was also tough. Test takers who fought their way through that passage would soon arrive at this brutal closer to the section. The science-based topic—embryo polarity, or how organisms determine what is up and down, and front and back—is unknown to most students, and certainly presented a reading challenge. The passage was then followed by eight questions, furthering the misery.
8. **June 2006, Passage #4: Maize**
   Maize is just another word for corn, so at first this passage doesn't look too difficult. Indeed, the first paragraph is

fairly easy to understand, as it lays out the importance of maize to the cultures that cultivated it. After the first paragraph, however, the discussion turns extremely detailed and covers the physical science behind why maize is so bountiful. Corn never tasted so bad.

9. **September 2006, Passage #4: Riddled Basins of Attraction**
   Similar to the Maize passage, the first paragraph of this passage is fairly easy to understand (it discusses the replication of experimental results in fairly clear terms). Thereafter, the passage discusses "riddled basins of attraction" and fractals as an analogy of systems where replicating results can be impossible. Those portions of the passage lead most students to feel that the passage was impossible.
10. **October 2008, Passage #3: Chinese Talk-story**
   This passage covers Maxine Hong Kingston and the literary antecedents of her writings in Chinese talk-stories. While the passage wasn't overly absorbing, the eight questions were where the real difficulty appeared, and many students struggled between two or more answers on more than one

occasion. Overall, after reading the passage, most students wanted nothing more to do with Kingston or her stories.

How to Prepare for LSAT Reading Comprehension

One great way to improve in the reading comprehension section is to read as much as possible! And when we say “read,” we aren’t talking about reading fashion magazines, sports digests, or romance novels. Since the Reading Comprehension section often asks you to look at multiple viewpoints and the logical structure behind the passage, you should look for articles that are written in layman's style but take positions or discuss complex ideas. The more you read ahead of time, the more comfortable you will be when you start doing actual LSAT Reading Comprehension passages.

Suggested Reading Material and the Proper Way to Approach the Material

Below we provide of list of publications that have been used as sources for information on past LSATs, as well as publications whose articles follow a format similar to the LSAT’s reading comprehension section:

Editorial and Opinion: The Editorial or Opinion pages of any major US Daily newspaper, such as the New York Times, the Washington Post, or the LA Times

Law, Politics, and Economics: Magazines such as Legal Affairs, The New Republic, The Atlantic Monthly, The Economist

History: The Journal of American History

Science: Magazines such as Scientific American, Popular Science

Once you have some reading material with which to practice, you can develop an effective strategy; below are some suggestions on how you should approach these materials.

- Your primary goal when starting an article is to find the main point. After every LSAT passage you will encounter questions that deal with the main point, so you need to develop the ability to quickly identify the main point of any material you read.
- In addition to the main point, you should be trying to put together a basic picture of the author—what is the author's perspective? Once you have identified the main point, your goal throughout the rest of the article is to identify the underlying logical structure of the passage. This will entail the following tasks:
    a. Identify any background thesis that may be challenged later in the article
    b. Identify any counterpoint(s) to the original thesis

c. Identify strengths and weaknesses of each viewpoint
d. Identify the author's ultimate conclusion and supporting premises

Writing Sample

At the end of your LSAT testing sessions, you will have 35 minutes to plan and write an essay on a given prompt. Even though your writing will not be scored, the sample *will* be sent to every law school to which you apply, along with your LSAT scores. Also, while there will be no low score to keep you out of a law school, law schools have are known to reject applicants who fail to respond to the prompt or who have done so in an impractical manner.

For the writing sample, they will ask you to choose between two courses of action or two positions on a problem. Your job will not be to make the "correct" choice, because there is not one. Defending both of the choices given is possible. You will, however, need to make a choice, support that choice well, and discredit the other choice with significant evidence.

Your writing for this sample will be limited to the front and back of a separate answer page. Keep in mind that the paper you submit will be duplicated and will be sent to law schools. Write neatly and stay within the space provided. Words written outside the lined space will not be duplicated.

Spending some time on this part of the LSAT would be to your advantage for several reasons. Doing well on it can boost your chances of law school acceptance and a poor response could harm them. It will be assumed by law schools that this sample is a true sign of your writing ability and it will be compared to other writing you submit. Additionally, law schools may use your performance on this essay to plan any remediation studies that are necessary to improve your writing. So, it is important to do your very best on this, as well as on other sections of the test.

Professionals in legal education validated and designed the LSAT writing sample prompt. The topics are generally of a non legal nature, but the type of writing being sought is much like that you will be required to do in law school. The Writing Sample is designed to check and test your ability to do these things:

- communicate effectively in written form
- write in an argumentative form that is common of writing required in law school

Writing Skills to Practice

As you practice writing in this format, make sure to ask the following questions about your work. It can be helpful to find a “study buddy” and take turns evaluating each other’s writing. This can give you some objective feedback.

<u>Reasoning</u>

- Have you supported each of your statements with given facts, evidence from the prompt, or frequently known information?

- Do the supporting facts clearly associate to your statements and are they sufficient to support them? If you cannot find enough relevant facts to support one side of the argument, you may need to switch on a different side. Remember, the purpose is not which side you take; it is how well you support it.

Clarity

Are your statements very clear to the reader? Avoid the use of overly long sentences in which the meaning becomes muddled. Try restructuring sentences so the meaning is more clear.

For example:

Clearly, the author, not being raised in this country and not having the knowledge of history here, was mistaken when he made the statement he did about the early settlers, and thus, his premise was misleading.

This text can be rewritten more clearly as follows:

Clearly, the author's premise concerning the early settlers was unfounded. This is probably due to his heritage, which failed to give background knowledge of this country's history.

Organization

Does your essay follow a logical sequence and are topics separated into paragraphs that answer one at a time? Before you start to write, you need to take a few minutes to plan or sketch out an outline of points you want to cover. Leave time at the end of the writing period to quickly review what you have written and correct any errors.

Language Usage

Did you use varied and pertinent language in expressing yourself? Sentences should be as descriptive as possible. Practice finding synonyms for typically overused words and learning the meanings of unfamiliar ones that could enrich your writing.

Examples:

Huge could become *expansive* or *tremendous* *amazing* could become *astonishing believable* could become *credible* or *convincing*

Mechanics

Are there capital letters and appropriate punctuation marks all over your piece? If you are at the point of applying to law school, you have surely been taught all the basics concerning punctuation and capitalization. But in this age of texting and abbreviated written language, it is easy to stumble into the habit of omitting standard writing conventions. The LSAT writing sample is *not* a good time to let your memory slip on these.

Be very sure you know how to use:

- common but confusing words, like *your* and *you're*
- Different words that sound alike but are spelled differently, such as *role* and *roll*

Are all of the words in your document spelled correctly? If spelling has been one of your less-developed skills, take a little time to study and practice it. Finding a list of commonly misspelled words would be a good place to start. There are also some helpful (and fun) games online that can help you seem more adept to the readers of your essay. Some particular things on which to focus are:

- vowel order, such as *ie* and *ei*
- word endings like *ing* and what happens to the base word when they are added (does the consonant double, is the *e* dropped, etc.)
- what happens to words when you include certain prefixes or suffixes

Legibility

At the present time, we tend to depend on keyboarding skills more than handwriting acumen to communicate. If you don't have a habit of actually writing with a pen, this would be a good time to practice. Be sure your letters are clear and that you leave spaces between words and between the lines. If the person who receives your essay cannot read it, all that great writing will be worthless.

One More Tip

Be very careful when responding to the given prompt. If you choose not to write to the prompt, your work will be discredited by the very people you want to accept you into their school.

Introduction to 10 Essential Grammar Rules for LSAT Writing

The format for the LSAT Writing and Language Test has undergone a series of changes by the College

Board. It's test format and structure resembles that of the ACT English Test, which means most students prepare for both at the same time. However, most students still feel intimidated with the LSAT Writing Session. To assist you with this monstrous-like section, put together top ten vital grammar rules to employ in the course of your LSAT Writing and Language Test. By reviewing, practicing, and memorizing these rules, you've just done yourself a favor as you draw closer to attaining the score you set for yourself

1. There Must be an Agreement between the Subject and Verb

The subject-verb agreement is arguably one of the most frequently used means of testing rules of grammar in the LSAT Writing Section. In short, if its a singular subject (one), it should have a singular verb, while for a plural subject (more than one), it should have a plural verb. A typical example is given below:

Singular: Jack runs down the street. (Jack is a singular subject, and runs is a singular verb)

Plural: Jack and Jill ran down the street. (Jack and Jill is a plural subject, and run is a plural verb)

If the difficulty level of each teach test question is so low as this, every student will pass with flying colors, but test-makers of LSAT like to make things complex a bit especially for this type of question. This brings us to the second rule.

2. Collective Nouns are Singular

To elaborate the basic subject-verb agreement, the LSAT Writing and Language Test often uses things like collective nouns to trick test-takers. For LSAT review, always remember that group words used to refer to multiple individuals are singular subjects. For example,

Incorrect: The jury are convinced that John is guilty.

Even though the subject jury refers to more than one person, as a collective noun, we take jury as a singular subject.

Correct: The jury is convinced that John is responsible or guilty.

Other examples of other collective nouns to look out for are: team, group, committee, crowd, class, and panel. Take note that multiple groups (panels, juries, groups, etc.) are used with plural verbs.

3. Prepositional Phrases

DO NOT Make a Subject Singular or Plural
One of the most crucial grammar rules to remember when doing prep for the LSAT Writing and Language Test is prepositions are not used when identifying whether or not a subject is plural or singular. Rather, the head noun, or the noun being modified, tells us which verb form to use. Examples of how the LSAT uses prepositions are,

Incorrect: The group of members are extremely passionate.

Correct: The group of members is very passionate.

Incorrect: The book which has five chapters are well written.

Correct: The book with five chapters is so satisfying.

As you can see, if you cross out the prepositional phrase altogether, you can easily identify the subject. In the stress and rush of taking the SATs, prepositional phrases can and might distract test takers from simple grammatical errors. By skipping the prepositional phrase, we quickly simplify the sentence and make the errors more apparent.

<u>4. Pronouns Must be Clear in Reference and Number</u>

On the LSAT Writing and Language Test, you have to always circle a pronoun and draw an arrow to the exact person, place, or thing being referenced. In your LSAT review, make sure to practice connecting pronouns to their nouns. For example,

Although John was tired, he still went running.

Here, we can see that the he being referenced is John. To check your ability to identify proper pronoun usage, the LSAT Writing and Language test often employs ambiguous pronouns (pronouns in the presence of more than one possible noun):

Incorrect: John, Jim, and Carl were running when he got exhausted and stopped.

Since there is more than one possible he, we cannot logically deduce who got tired and stopped. Instead, a right or correct answer would be one that specifies a specific individual.

Correct: John,Jim, and Carl were running when Jim got exhausted and stopped.

Along with using ambiguous pronouns to test your knowledge, the LSAT employs sentences in which the pronoun does not agree with the number of nouns being referenced.

Incorrect: The mile times of the students in Jim's class were greater than that of Carl's class.

As we understood above, prepositional phrases do not make a subject singular or plural. Here, we skip the prepositional phrase to clearly see that the pronoun that is used in reference to the noun mile times. Since mile times are a plural subject, the pronoun is also plural. To correct the error, the sentence should read:

Correct: The mile times of the students in Jim's class were greater than those of Carl's class.

When you review for the LSAT Language and Writing Test, always remember that I, me, you, she, her, it, and him are singular and we, us, you, they, and them are plural. To make it much easier on yourself, whenever you see a pronoun in a question, circle it in the text and draw an arrow to the noun it's referring to.

5. Modifiers have to Appear Next to Whatever they're Modifying

The usual error type on the LSAT Writing Section is the use of dangling and misplaced modifiers. Precisely what they sound like, modifiers are words or phrases that modify another word to give the reader more information. In your LSAT Review, always remember that whenever you see a modifier, especially at the beginning of a sentence, remember that the word directly following the comma must be the word being modified. Errors would typically be as follows,

Incorrect: A very bright young boy, engineering came easily to Billy.

Because the word being modified has to appear directly after the modifier, the modifying phrase (A very precocious young boy) is incorrectly referring to computer engineering. To fix the error, the sentence should read,

Correct: A very bright young boy, Billy found engineering easy.

Along with these modifiers at the beginning of a sentence, the LSAT Writing and Language Test commonly uses modifiers in incorrect or ambiguous positions. For example,

Incorrect: The basketball player told everyone about his plans to train harder during the meeting.

In this incorrect usage, the modifying phrase (during the meeting) is placed in a position that causes inconclusiveness. Is the basketball player going to train harder during that certain meeting? Is he going to train harder during the season? To correct the error, we need to move the modifier to clarify what really is happening.

Correct: During the meeting, the basketball player told everyone about his plans to train harder.

Here, we can clearly see that the basketball player is the word being modified, and he aims to train harder in general, rather than at the meeting. Because of idiomatically we often believe both sentences as the same thing, it is especially important to pay close attention to the use of modifiers during the LSAT Writing and Language Test and during your LSAT Writing preparation. You always have to be able to circle a modifier and draw an arrow to the exact word being modified. If you can't, you need to select the answer choice that makes it absolutely clear.

6. Each Word Should Make Sense in Context

More to the joy of test-takers everywhere, the dreaded vocabulary section present on old LSAT tests is gone for good. While this means you don't have to memorize five hundred obscure words a day, you still need to have a good understanding of medium-difficulty words. Just like the ACT English Test, the LSAT Writing and Language Test uses word choice questions that will challenge your knowledge of things like homophones (words that sound similar, but have different meanings) and words that have multiple definitions. Be sure to spend some time in your LSAT Writing prep to study essential words and commonly used homophones.

For homophone questions, the sentence will typically read something like:

There are a number of dogs without their collars.

A) NO CHANGE
B) There, their (Correct Answer)
C) Their, there
D) They're, their

For word choice questions, the sentence will sometimes look like:

Despite the fact that fitness advocates preserve that the supplement is beneficial, the FDA has yet to release positive results.

A) NO CHANGE
B) sustain
C) maintain (Correct Answer)

D) endure

Keep in mind, during the real LSAT and ACT, these sentences will appear in a longer passage. Even though sentences like these supply you with the context you need to answer the question, you need to read the overall tone and message of the passage to understand which definition works best. Because LSAT test makers presume you will be in a hurry, they create answer choices that are correct definitions of the word but are not appropriate for the sentence. Always select your answers in the greater context of the sentence and passage.

7. Commas Separate Main and Subordinate Clauses

A sentence contains a subject and a predicate. Put more simply, a noun and a verb phrase. The LSAT Writing and Language test likes to challenge your knowledge of what constitutes a sentence with something called a comma splice. This occurs when two grammatically complete sentences are combined with just a comma. For example,

Incorrect: Pandas are my favorite animal, they are so cute.

Each of these statements includes a noun (Panda/They) and a verb statement (are my…/are so), and are therefore complete on their own. To correct the error, each main clause must be separated by a period, semicolon, or coordinating conjunction.

Correct: Pandas are my favorite animal. They are so cute.

Correct: Pandas are my favorite animal; they are so cute.

Correct: Pandas are my favorite animal, because they are so cute.

With this knowledge, we can better comprehend our next essential grammatical rule.

8. Follow Sentence Rules to Prevent Run-Ons and Fragments

Despite the fact that numerous people tend to associate run-ons with wordiness and fragments with shortness, both are simply just clauses that don't follow the grammatical rules for complete sentences. For a sentence to be accomplished, it needs to have at least one main clause (subject and predicate), and all main clauses must be connected with the proper punctuation. As seen in the previous rule, this means that main clauses must be connected by semicolons, or coordinating conjunctions and commas. Also, a sentence is a fragment if there is no main clause.

Run-On: My wife comes from the city and I come from the Suburbs.

Fragment: My wife coming from the city and I from the suburbs.

Correct: My wife comes from the city, and I come from the suburbs.

9. Verbs and Sentence Structure must Remain Parallel

To guarantee that a sentence is grammatically correct, all verb tenses and grammatical structures must remain parallel. Put simply, this means that words have to be repeated to maintain a pattern. As this is a very frequent error type, be sure to practice it for your LSAT Writing Prep. In terms of word choice, an example that may happen on the LSAT is:

Incorrect: John is planning to buy a new car, partly because of his need to have a reliable vehicle, but mostly because of his greatly desiring to look cool.

Correct: John planning to buy a new car, partly because of his need to have a reliable vehicle, but mostly because of his desire to look cool.

As you can see in the first example, the sentence is linked with the conjunction but and the phrase because of is repeated. To always maintain the parallel structure, the noun phrase his greatly wanting has to match the noun phrase structure of his need. Along with word structure, verb tense must stay consistent throughout the sentence.

Incorrect: John loved running with his friends, swimming in the ocean, and walk through the valley.

Correct: John loved running with his friends, swimming in the ocean, and walking through the valley.

10. <u>Correlative Coordination Means Two Parts</u>
One of the most common, but easiest error-types to know is the use of a coordinator without its matching word. Because the first coordinator needs its pair word to be complete, you should circle the word anytime you see it and quickly identify if its partner word is present in the sentence.

..or – Either John or Jim both are the club leader.
..and – Both John and Jim are funny.
not so much…as – He's not so much funny as he is annoying.

just as…so
..nor
not only…but(also)
at once…and

LSAT Vocabulary

As you are by this point most certainly aware, the LSAT is full of complex and unusual words and phrases. However, as we've discussed many times, when it comes time to answer questions, it is the small, common words between those unusual ones—the common words that define reasoning relationships—that are most important. We've been highlighting many of these important reasoning words throughout the book. In this lesson, we're going to take a quick break from Logical Reasoning to have a concentrated lesson just on LSAT vocabulary. And, not so coincidentally, I hope you find the work we do in this lesson helpful as you conquer Inference questions in the next one.

When it comes to mastering LSAT vocabulary, there are two different aspects to consider:

Understanding the Words Correctly

Duh. The good news is that nearly all of the important terms are easy and simple to understand. The bad news is that certain terms are very easy to misunderstand no matter how much you prepare. Oftentimes, getting a question correct requires that we translate and utilize many different words in a very short amount of time—your understanding of most key terms needs to be absolute and automatic; furthermore, you need to have a good sense of which words tend to cause you trouble, and you want to make sure you have systems for dealing with these terms.

Prioritizing Key Terms

This second issue is of far more importance than the first. These key terms shape reasoning structure and reasoning relationships—the two things LSAT questions happen to be about. Students who perform poorly, or who spend far more time than they should, invariably waste energy focusing on the wrong parts of an argument or a passage. The main reason I've put this lesson is not to remind you of what words mean, but rather to remind you of which words to pay attention to.

Terminology

Of course, it's not the easy words that worry most people. It's the sudden or anticipated words, or terms we've never seen that cause the most concern. In my view, these types of challenging LSAT vocabulary terms becomes these three distinct categories:

- Advanced words
- Scientific or technical jargon
- Logical terminology

Let's look at each group in more detail.

Advanced Words

By “advanced words,” I mean the high-level vocabulary words that you rarely encounter in a day to day basis. Examples (not from the LSAT) would include words such as “tenebrous”1 or “recondite.”2 Those are words that you just don’t hear in your general conversations with your friends, classmates, or coworkers! Fortunately, words at this high of a level are extremely rare on the LSAT, and even the hardest general vocabulary words to appear on the test are more on the level of words like “eschew” or “flouted” (both of which have been used on the LSAT).

When considering what vocab level is required for a strong LSAT performance, let’s consider what the test makers have to say about the issue. As stated in LSAC, the makers of the LSAT, “Usually, the selections are densely written, use high-level vocabulary, and contain sophisticated argument or complex rhetorical structure (for example, multiple conclusions).3” Additionally, “These questions assess the ability to analyze, critically evaluate, and complete arguments as they occur in ordinary language.” So, there is an expectation of a high-level vocabulary, but there is no exact definition as to what that means, and certainly no published list of words that constitute a high-level vocabulary.

Therefore, should you study a list of hard vocab words in preparation for the LSAT? The answer is no. First, you’d likely be wasting a huge amount of time preparing for words that you most likely wouldn’t see on the test. Second, there is a bright side when difficult vocabulary is used: in practice, when this happens, LSAT authors generally either define the word or provide sufficient context in the passage to determine what the word means. For instance, an LSAT question about scientific discoveries that used the word “serendipity” immediately followed that usage by giving the definition of that word as “the chance discovery of precious findings.”Because of that, even without knowing the meaning of serendipity, you could still easily complete the question. One more example, an LSAT question utilizes used the word “duplicitous,” but before that usage had described the behavior of the individuals in question in a way that made it clear that “dishonest” meant “deceptive” or “deceitful.” The bottom line is that in many instances, when you encounter what would be termed as high-level vocabulary, there will be information around that method that helps you to understand the meaning of the word.

Scientific/Technical/Legal Jargon

Specialized terminology can be among the terrifying vocabulary you encounter on the LSAT. Seeing terms such as “amygdala,” “thermovoltaic generators,” or “tangible-object theory” will cause most test takers to pause for a moment. But despite that, these types of specialized terms are beyond the general vocabulary of almost every LSAT taker, and thus, LSAC does not presume you will know the meaning of such terms. In each instance, a description will be supplied in the passage (as was the case in all three instances mentioned above). While this description is often in the immediate vicinity of the first appearance of the word, in some cases (notably in Reading Comprehension) the definition is provided a number of lines later. Anyhow, when you find terms of this type, start looking for the definition that will most certainly be provided (and relax, because you won’t have to guess at the meaning of the word).

Note that one of the usual tricks of the test makers is to place an ominous looking word before a more commonly understood concept. For example, when the phrase "Streptococcus bacteria" was used on the LSAT, no definition was given. Of course, the test makers anticipate everyone to understand the basic ideas behind bacteria, and the question itself did not hinge on any specific knowledge relating to Streptococcus. However, there was no need for an exact discussion of that particular type of bacteria.

Logical Terminology

Even if the LSAT does not require you to comprehend specific terms from the scientific, medical, technical, or legal worlds, many LSAT questions are based on your knowledge of certain words or phrases that are portion of the logical canon of the test. Most of the words that present problems are not comprehensive logic terms, however. As LSAC indicates, "The questions do not presume specialized knowledge of logical terminology. For example, you will not be required to know the meaning of specialized terms such as 'ad hominem' or 'syllogism.'"

Instead, the words and phrases that created problems on the LSAT tend to be those that are defined in a way that differs from their more common, "real world" definitions. These particular words, such as "some" or "either…or," appear innocent but can cause serious problems if misinterpreted during the exam. Because even a single missed question can drop your scaled LSAT score by one point, LSAT students must know the exact definitions of the logical terms that LSAC uses frequently.

The bottom line is regardless of the fact that the LSAT is not a direct test of your vocabulary, there is an expectation that you have at least a solid vocabulary, and that you fully understand the usage of certain common terms such as "conclusion" or "correlation." You do not have to worry about knowing very specialized terminology, and the definitions of high-level words you run into will often be easy to deduce based on context. So, set aside that vocab list and instead spend your time studying argumentation and Logic Games!

Pay Attention to These Terms on Your Test

Some (and other quantity indicator words)

Words like "some" are commonly understood to mean 2-3 of anythings. But on the LSAT, it particularly means "at least one." Take a look at this example. Imagine on the test, you read:

"Some of the tests were misprinted." You should know that, on the LSAT, this means "at least one of the tests was misprinted." When dealing with the logical reasoning section, make sure to know this particular meaning of "some," and know that its logical opposite is "none." The same goes for other quantity indicators like "most, all, few" etc.

Follows

The word "follows" can sometimes be found in the logical reasoning section. You'll see it in questions like, "Which one of the following choices follows logically from the passage?"

As usual, "follows" means "comes after" or "results." But when we're dealing with logic on the LSAT, we should look at this word more strictly. Especially on must be true questions, you'll be checking to see if you can logically conclude an idea based on connecting logical statements.

Often on must be true questions, the conclusion that "follows" could be found by connecting conditional statements. Or, it's the contrapositive of the original statements.

At Least

On the LSAT, particularly within the logic games section, be aware for the phrase "at least." In grouping games, for example, you might find a sentence like, "At least two people operate in the purple group." If you read that too quickly, you might read it simply as, "Two people work in the purple group." Of course, this can lead to lots of trouble when you reach a question that asks, "What is the maximum number of people who can work in the purple group?" At first, you probably think to yourself, "Two is the obvious answer, why are they asking about a maximum?" Then, late in the game, you'll be aware of the fact that you skipped over that dreaded phrase "at least!"

Keep in mind that "at least" means at that level or beyond.

Terms to Know

The following is a list of high frequency vocabulary words commonly found on the LSATS

Aberrant: deviating from the norm

aberrant: Markedly different from an accepted norm.
aberration: Deviation from a right, usual, or recommended course.
abeyance: A state of suspension or temporary inaction.
abjure: To recant, renounce, repudiate under oath.
ablution: A washing or cleansing, particularly of the body.
abrogate: To abolish, repeal.
Abscond: run away secretly
abscond: To leave secretly and suddenly for the goal of escaping arrest.
abstemious: Portrayed by self denial or abstinence, as in the use of drink, food.
Abstract: theoretical or to summarize or a summary
abstruse: Dealing with matters difficult to be understood.
abut: To tap at the end or boundary line.
accede: To agree.
Accelerate: speed up
Acculturate: to adapt to a culture
acquiesce: To comply; submit.
acrid: Harshly pungent or bitter.

acumen: Quickness of perception, intellectual insight or; keenness of discrimination.
adage: An old saying.
adamant: Any substance of exceeding hardness or impenetrability.
Adamant: hard, unyielding, very hard stone
Adjourn: to suspend, as a meeting
admonition: Gentle reproof.
Adulation: admiration
adumbrate: To represent beforehand in outline or by symbol.
Aerate: to supply or combine with oxygen or air
Aesthetic: artistic, relating to beauty
affable: Easy to approach.
Affable: friendly, pleasant
Affiliation: connecting, association
Affluent: wealthy
Aggrandize: praise greatly, make seem greater
aggrandize: To cause to appear greatly.
aggravate: To make heavier, worse, or more burdensome.
agile: Able to act or move quickly, mentally or physically.
agog: In eager desire.

alacrity: Cheerful willingness.
Alacrity: promptness, eagerness
alcove: A covered recess linked with or at the side of a larger room.
alleviate: To make less hard to bear or less burdensome.
Alloy: mixture esp of metal
Allusive: referring to or hinting to something esp in literature
aloof: Not in sympathy with or hoping to associate with others.
Altruism: unselfish behavior
amalgamate: To blend or mix together in a homogeneous body.
ambidextrous: Having the ability to utilize both hands with equal skill or ease.
ambiguous: Having a double meaning.
Ambivalent: uncertain, having conflicting feelings
Amble: walk leisurely
ameliorate: To relieve, as from pain or hardship
Amenable: agreeable, obedient
Amorphous: without shape, unclassifiable
Anachronism: a thing or person out of place in time
anathema: Anything forbidden, as by social usage.

animadversion: The utterance of criticism or censure.
animosity: Hatred.
Anomalous: irregular, unusual
Antagonism: hostility, enmity
antediluvian: Of or referring to the things, times, events before the great flood happened in the days of Noah.
antidote: Anything that will remove or counteract the effects of poison, disease, or the like.
Antipathy: strong feeling against, dislike for
Antithesis: direct opposite
aplomb: Confidence; coolness.
apocryphal : Of doubtful authority or authenticity.
Apocryphal: spurious, not genuine
apogee: The climax.
apostate: False.
apotheosis: Deification.
apparition: Ghost.
appease: To soothe by quieting anger or indignation.
apposite: Appropriate.
Apposite: relevant, to the point
apprise: To give notice to; to inform.

Approbation: praise, approval
approbation: Sanction.
Arbitrary: random, capricious, impartial
arboreal: Of or concerning to a tree or trees.
Arcane: secret, esoteric
ardor: Intensity of passion or affection.
Arduous: difficult, strenuous
argot: A specialized vocabulary peculiar to a particular group.
Arid: dry
arrant: Notoriously bad.
Arrogant: overbearing, proud
Articulate: well- spoken, intelligible, speak clearly and distinctly
Artlessness: crudeness, naturalness
Ascetic: austere, disciplined
ascetic: Given to extreme self-denial and practicing excessive abstinence and devotion.
ascribe: To assign as a quality or attribute.
asperity: Harshness or roughness of temper.
Aspiration: hope, ambition, breathing in
Assert: to state without need of proof
assiduous: Unceasing; persistent

assuage: To cause to be less violent, harsh, or severe, as excitement, appetite, pain, or disease.
astringent: Harsh in disposition or character.
astute: Keen in discernment.
atonement: Amends, expiation, or reparation made from wrong or injury.
audacious: Fearless.
augury: Omen
auspicious: Favorable omen
austere: Severely simple; unadorned.
Authentic: genuine, trustworthy
autocrat: Any one who exerts or claims undisputed or unrestricted authority or influence.
auxiliary: One who or that which helps or aids, especially when regarded as subsidiary or accessory.
Avarice: greed
avarice: Passion for getting and keeping riches.
aver: To avouch, justify or prove
aversion: A mental condition of fixed resistance to or dislike of a certain thing.
Avert: turn away, avoid
avow: To declare openly.
baleful: Malignant.
banal: Commonplace.

bask: To make warm by genial heat.
beatify: To make supremely happy.
bedaub: To smear over, as with something oily or slimy.
Belie: contradict, give false cover to
bellicose: Warlike.
belligerent: Manifesting a warlike spirit.
benefactor: A doer of kindly and charitable acts.
benevolence: Any act of kindness or well-doing.
benign: Good and kind of heart.
berate: To scold severely.
bet: To support, encourage, promote or the commission of (an offense).
bewilder: To confuse the perceptions or judgment of.
blandishment: Flattery intended to persuade.
blatant: Noisily or offensively loud or clamorous.
blithe: Joyous.
boisterous: Unchecked merriment or animal spirits.
Bolster: support
bolster: To support, as something wrong.
bombast: Inflated or extravagant vocabulary, especially on insignificant subjects.

Bombast: pompous speech
boorish: Rude.
breach: The violation of official duty, lawful obligation, or lawful right.
brittle: Fragile.
broach: To mention, for the first time.
Bucolic: pastoral, relating to country life
bumptious: Full of offensive and aggressive self-conceit.
buoyant: Having the power or keep afloat or tendency to float.
Burgeon: to bloom, flourish
burnish: To make brilliant or shining.
Buttress: supporting piece of a structure, strengthen, support
cabal: A total volume of persons secretly united for effecting by intrigue some private purpose.
cacophony: A harsh, disagreeable, or discordant sound or combination of sounds or tones.
cajole: To rely on or dupe by flattering speech.
callow: Without experience of the world.
calumny: Slander.
candid: Straightforward.
Candor: straightforwardness, sincerity

cant: To talk in a singsong, preaching tone with affected solemnity.
capacious: Roomy.
capitulate: To surrender or stipulate terms.
capitulate:give in, surrender
Caprice: impulsive action, whim
captious: Hypercritical.
Carrion: animal remains
Castigate: scold severely
castigate: To punish.
Catalyst: a thing that sets another in motion or causes change
cataract: Opacity of the lens of the eye resulting in partial or complete blindness.
caustic: Sarcastic and severe.
Censure: disapprove, condemn, disapproval, condemnation
censure: To criticize severely; also, an expression of dissatisfaction.
centurion: A captain of a company of 100 hundred infantry in the ancient Roman army.
Cessation: stoppage, ceasing
chagrin: Keen vexation, annoyance, or mortification, as at one's failures or errors.
Charade: pretense

chary: Careful; wary; cautious.
Chauvinist: extreme patriot, one who believes one group is superior to another
Chicanery: flim-flam, trickery
chicanery: The use of trickery to deceive.
Circuitous: round-about, indirect
Circumlocution: excessive speaking, wordiness
circumlocution: Indirect or roundabout expression.
Cloying: sweet, sentimental
coddle: To consider as invalid or a baby.
coerce: To force.
coeval: Existing during the same timeline; also, a contemporary.
cogent: Appealing strongly to the reason or conscience.
cogitate: Consider carefully and deeply; ponder.
Cogitate: to think hard, ponder
cognizant: Taking notice.
Coherent: intelligible, consistent
Collaborate: to work together, cooperate
colloquial: Peculiar or pertaining to common speech as prominent from literary.
collusion: A secret agreement for a wrongful purpose.

Colossus: giant statue, very large thing
comestible: Fit to be eaten.
commemorate: To serve as a remembrance of.
Commodious: having ample space
complaisance: Politeness.
complement: To make complete.
Component: essential element
comport: To conduct or behave (oneself).
Comprehensive: all inclusive
compunction: Remorseful feeling.
Concede: to yield, grant
conceit: Self-flattering opinion.
conciliatory: Tending to reconcile.
Concise: exact
concord: Harmony.
Concur: agree
concur: To agree.
condense: To abridge.
conflagration: A huge fire, as of many buildings, a forest, or the like.
Conflate: to blend together, esp a text
confluence: The place where streams meet.

Conform: adapt or compliant with
congeal: To coagulate.
conjoin: To unite.
Connive: to conspire, to be in secret sympathy with
connoisseur: A crucial judge of art, especially one with in-depth knowledge and sound judgment of art.
Connoisseur: one who appreciates fine things
console: To comfort.
Consolidate: to join together, merge
conspicuous: Clearly visible.
consternation: Panic.
Constrain: restrict, confine
constrict: To bind.
Constrict: to compress, constract
Consummate: complete, accomplish, perfect, to a high degree
consummate: To bring to completion.
Contend: fight with,oppose
Contigeous: adjacent with, borders touching
contiguous: Touching or joining the edge or boundary.
contrite: Discouraged in spirit because of a sense of sin.

Contrite: sorry, repentant
contumacious: Rebellious.
Conundrum: riddle, puzzle
Converge: come together, merge
Convoluted: intricate, coiled, twisted
copious: Plenteous.
cornucopia: The horn of abundant, symbolizing prosperity and peace.
corporeal: Of a material nature; physical.
correlate: To put in some correspondence or relation of alliance.
Correspond: to match, to conform, to parallel
Corroborate: to confirm or make certain
corroboration: Confirmation.
Countenance: face, expression or allow to happen
counterfeit: Made to resemble something else.
countervail: To offset.
covert: Concealed, especially for an evil purpose.
cower: To crouch down startled, as through fear or shame.
crass: Coarse or thick in nature or structure, as opposed to thin or fine.
credulous: Easily deceived.

Crusade: a zealous campaign for a cause
Cryptic: encoded, secret, indecipherable
Culpable: deserving of blame
cupidity: Avarice.
cursory: Rapid and superficial.
curtail: To cut off or cut short.
Cyclical: periodic and repeating
Cynic: one who has an attitude of contempt, distrust
cynosure: That to which main interest or attention is directed.
Daunt: subdue or tame
dearth: Scarcity, as of something customary, essential,or desirable.
Decorous: in good taste, very proper
Defer: to postpone or to submit to another
defer: To put off or delay to some other time.
Definitive: authoritative
deign: To deem worthy of notice or account.
deleterious: Hurtful, morally or physically.
delineate: To represent by sketch or diagram.
deluge: To overwhelm with a flood of water.
demagogue: An unprincipled politician.

Demise: death, cessation
Demur: to hesitate, protest
denizen: Inhabitant.
denouement: That part of a play or story in which the mystery is clarified.
deplete: To minimize or reduce, as by use, exhaustion, or waste.
Depletion: lessening
deposition: Testimony legally taken on interrogatories and minimized to writing, for use as evidence in court.
deprave: To render bad, especially morally bad.
deprecate: To show regret or disapproval with the hope for the opposite.
deride: To ridicule.
derision: Ridicule.
Derision: scorning, ridicule
derivative: Coming or acquired from some origin.
descry: To discern.
desiccant: Any cure which, when applied externally, absorbs moisture or dries up, as that of wounds.
Desiccate: to dry out, dehydrate
desuetude: A state of disuse or inactivity.
desultory: Not connected with what precedes.

deter: To frighten away.
dexterity: Readiness,efficiency, precision, and ease in any physical activity or in any mechanical work.
diaphanous: Transparent.
diatribe: A bitter or malicious criticism.
Dichotomy: separation into two parts
didactic: Pertaining to teaching.
diffidence: Self-distrust.
diffident: Affected or possessed with self-distrust.
Diffident: shy, reserved
Diffuse: to spread thinly, or scattered
Digress: to move away from
dilate: To enlarge in all directions.
dilatory: Tending to cause delay.
Dilettante: amateur, dabbler
Dimension: property of space, as in height, width, depth
disallow: To withhold permission or sanction.
Disarm: to deprive of weapons or to win over, ingratiate
discomfit: To put to confusion.
disconcert: To disturb the composure of.

disconsolate : Hopelessly sad; also, saddening; cheerless.
Discord: argument, strife
discountenance: To look upon with disfavor.
Discourse: conversation, long paper or speech on a subject
discredit: To injure the reputation of.
Discreet: having good judgment, prudent
discreet: Judicious.
Discrete: distinct, separate
disheveled: Disordered; disorderly; untidy.
Disingenuous: seemingly honest while not being so
Disperse: to spread out
Disquiet: disturb or upset
Dissemble: lie
dissemble: To hide by pretending something different.
disseminate: To scatter or sow abroad, as seed is sown.
dissent: Disagreement.
Dissent: to disagree
dissolution: A breaking up of an alliance of persons.
distraught: Bewildered.

Diverge: to go apart in different directions
divulge: To announce or tell, as something previously private or secret.
Doctrine: creed, belief
Dogma: firmly held disbelief
dogmatic: Making statements without argument or evidence.
Dormant: asleep, inactive
dormant: Being in a state or condition of sleep.
Dubious: doubtful, questionable
dubious: Doubtful.
duplicity: Double-dealing.
Dynamic: in motion
earthenware: Everything made of clay and baked in a kiln or dried in the sun.
ebullient: Showing enthusiasm or exhilaration of feeling.
Eccentric: unusual, strange
Eclectic: having varying elements
Eclipse: overshadowing, esp sun or moon
edacious: Given to eating.
edible: Suitable to be eaten.
educe: To draw out.

effete: Exhausted, as having performed its functions.
efficacy: The power to generate an intended effect as shown in the production of it.
Effrontery: boldness
effrontery: Unblushing impudence.
effulgence: Splendor.
egregious: Extreme.
egress: Any place of exit.
Egress: exit
elegy: A lyric poem lamenting the dead.
elicit: To extract or induce gradually or without violence.
Ellipse: oval
Elucidate: make clear, explain
elucidate: To bring out more clearly the essentials concerning.
Elusive: difficult to find or pin down
emaciate: To waste away in flesh.
embellish: To make elegant or appealing by adding attractive or ornamental features.
embezzle: To misappropriate secretly.
emblazon: To express publicly or in glowing terms.
Emollient: lotion that moisturizes

encomium: A formal or discriminating expression of praise.
encumbrance: A burdensome and troublesome load.
endemic: Peculiar to some specified country or people.
Endow: to grant, as a gift
enervate: To render ineffective or inoperative.
Engender: to create, foster
engender: To produce.
engrave: To cut or carve in or onto some surface.
enigma: A riddle.
enmity: Hatred.
entangle: To involve in difficulties, confusion, or complications.
entreat: To ask for or request earnestly.
Enumerate: to count
Ephemeral: fleeting, or short life or duration
Epicurean:Pertaining, ministering, or indulging to daintiness of appetite.
epithet: Word used adjectivally to describe some quality or attribute of is objects, as in “Father Aeneas”.
epitome: A simplified representation.
equable: Equal and uniform; also, serene.

equanimity : Calmness; composure.
equanimity: Evenness of mind or temper.
equilibrium: A state of balance.
Equilibrium: state of balance
equivocal: Ambiguous.
Equivocal: wavering, vacillating
equivocate: To use words of double meaning.
eradicate: To destroy thoroughly.
Eradicate: to eliminate completely
errant: Roaming or nomadic, in search of adventure or opportunity for gallant deeds.
Errant: wandering, traveling
erratic: Irregular.
erroneous: Incorrect.
erudite: Very-learned.
Erudition: knowledge, esp gained from books
eschew: To keep clear of.
Esoteric: hidden, available only to the initiate
Espouse: to take to oneself, to adopt a belief
espy: To keep close watch.
eulogy: A spoken or written distinction of a person's life or character.

Euphemism: mild word or phrase substituted for an offensive one
euphonious: Characterized by agreeableness of sound.
evanescent: Fleeting.
evince: To make manifest or evident.
evoke: To call or summon forth.
Exacerbate: aggravate, make worse
exacerbate: To make more sharp, severe, or virulent.
exculpate: To relieve of blame.
exhaustive: Thorough and complete in execution.
exigency : State of requiring urgent action; also, an urgent situation; also, that which is required in a
exigency: A critical period or condition.
Exigent: needing swift action
exorbitant: Going beyond usual and proper limits.
expatiate: To speak or write at some length.
expedient: Contributing to personal advantage.
Expend: to use up
expiate: To make satisfaction or amends for.
explicate: To clear from involvement.
expostulate: To discuss.

expropriate: To transfer (another's property) to oneself, also, to deprive of possession.
extant: Still existing and known.
extempore: Without studied or special preparation.
Extemporize: to speak spontaneously
extenuate: To diminish the gravity or importance of.
extinct: Being no longer in existence.
extinguish: To render extinct.
extirpate: To root out; to eradicate.
extol: To praise in the highest terms.
extort: To obtain by violence, threats, compulsion, or the subjection of another to some necessity.
extraneous: Having no essential relation to a subject.
exuberance: Rich supply.
Fabricate: to create
Facade: false front
facetious: Amusing.
facile: Not difficult to do.
factious: Turbulent.
fallacious: Illogical.
Fallacy: a logical flaw, mistake

Fallow: barren, not cultivated or sown
Falter: stumble, hesitate
Fatuous: foolish, silly
fatuous: Idiotic
fawn: A young deer.
Feign: to pretend
feint: Any sham, pretense, or deceptive movement.
Felicity: happiness, pleasantness
felon: A criminal or depraved person.
ferocity: Savageness.
Ferrous: with iron
fervid: Intense.
fervor: Ardor or intensity of feeling.
Fickle: changeable, not constant
fidelity: Loyalty.
finesse: Subtle contrivance used to gain a point.
Flaccid: limp, drooping
Flagrant: bold, open, apparent
flamboyant: Described by exciting and in general by want of good taste.
Fledging: young, inexperienced
flippant: Having a light, pert, trifling disposition.

Florid: flowery or reddish
florid: Flushed with red.
flout: To treat with contempt.
Fluctuate: vary widely
foible: A personal weakness or failing.
foment: To inspire back to life or activity; to encourage.
foppish: Characteristic of someone who is too immensely devoted to dress and the niceties of manners.
Forage: look for food
forbearance: Patient endurance or toleration of offenses.
forfeit: To lose control through failure to fulfill some obligation.
forgery: Counterfeiting.
forswear: To renounce upon oath.
Fracas: riot, flight
fragile: Easily broken.
frantic: Frenzied.
frugal: Economical.
fugacious: Fleeting.
fulminate: To cause to explode.
fulsome: Offensive from excess of praise or commendation.

Furtive: secret, sneaky
Fusion: merging of diverse parts into a whole
gainsay: To contradict; to deny.
gamut: The whole range or sequence.
Garrulous: extremely talkative
garrulous: Given to constant trivial talking.
germane: Relevant.
gesticulate: To make signs or gestures, as in speaking, or in place of speech.
Gist: general meeting, essence
glimmer: A faint, wavering, unsteady light.
gossamer: Flimsy.
gourmand: An expert in the delicacies of the table.
Gourmand: one who likes to eat alot
Grandiloquent: having high sounding speech
grandiloquent: Speaking in or characterized by a arrogant or bombastic style.
Gratuitous: uncalled for, not warranted
Gregarious: outgoing, friendly
gregarious: Sociable, outgoing
grievous: Creating affliction.
Guile: cunning, trickery

guile: Duplicity.
gullible: Credulous.
halcyon: Calm.
Halcyon: happy, prosperous, peaceful
Hallmark: distinguishing mark
harangue: A tirade.
Harangue: long, complaining speech
harbinger: One who or that which foreruns and announces the coming of any person or thing.
head: Adv. Precipitately, as in diving.
Hedonist: one who lives for pleasure
heinous: Odiously sinful.
heresy: An opinion or doctrine subversive of settled beliefs or accepted principles.
Heretic: one who holds unorthodox or unapproved beliefs
heterogeneous: Consisting of dissimilar elements or ingredients of different kinds.
Heterogeneous: mixed, made up of unlike elements
hirsute: Having a hairy covering.
hoodwink: To deceive.
hospitable: Disposed to treat strangers or guests with generous kindness.
Hydrate: add water

Hyperbole: excessive exaggeration
hypocrisy: Extreme insincerity.
iconoclast: An image-breaker.
Ideology: set of beliefs
idiosyncrasy: A mental quality or habit peculiar to an individual.
ignoble: Low in character or purpose.
ignominious: Shameful.
illicit: Unlawful.
imbroglio: A misunderstanding attended by ill feeling, perplexity, or strife.
imbue : To dye; to instill profoundly.
immaculate: Without spot or blemish.
imminent: Dangerous and close at hand.
immutable: Unchangeable.
impair: To cause to become less or worse.
Impalpable: not physical, not able to be touched
impassive: Unmoved by or not exhibiting feeling.
impecunious: Having no money.
impede: To be an obstacle or to place obstacles in the way of.
Impenetrable: unable to penetrate, pierced
Imperative: necessary, immediately important

imperative: Obligatory.
imperious: Insisting on obedience.
imperturbable: Calm.
impervious: Impenetrable.
impetuous: Impulsive.
impiety: Irreverence toward God.
implacable: Incapable of being pacified.
Implacable: not able to be changed
Implausible: not believable
implicate: To show or prove to be involved in or concerned
Implicit: implied, tacitly understood
implicit: Implied.
importunate: Urgent in character, request, or demand.
importune: To harass with persistent demands or entreaties.
impromptu: Anything done or said on the impulse of the moment.
Impromptu: spontaneous, spur of the moment
improvident: Lacking foresight or thrift.
impugn: To assail with arguments, insinuations, or accusations.
Impunity: without fear of punishment

impute: To attribute.
Inadvertence: oversight, unwillingness
inadvertent: Accidental.
Inane: silly, empty-headed
inane: Silly.
incessant: Unceasing.
inchoate: Incipient.
Incipient: beginning, budding
incipient: Initial.
incite: To rouse to a particular action.
Incompatible: not well matched, unsuited
incongruous: Unsuitable for the time, place, or occasion.
Incubation: period of gestation
inculcate: To teach by frequent repetitions.
indelible: That can not be blotted out, effaced, destroyed, or removed.
Indictment: formal charge against a person
indigence: Poverty.
Indigenous: native, originating in a place
indigenous: Native.
indistinct: Vague.
indolence: Laziness.

indolent: Habitually inactive or idle.
indomitable: Unconquerable.
indulgent: Yielding to the desires or humor of oneself or those under one's care.
ineffable: Unutterable.
ineluctable: Impossible to avoid.
inept: Not fit or suitable.
inexorable: Unrelenting.
Inextricable: not able to be untangled
infuse: To instill, introduce, or inculcate, as principles or qualities.
Ingenious: extremely clever, original
ingenuous: Candid, frank, or open in character or quality.
Inherent: in the essential nature of a thing
Inhibit: restrain, forbid
inimical: Adverse.
innocuous: Harmless.
Inopportune: not timely, inappropriate
Inquisitive: curious, seeking knowledge
inscrutable: Impenetrably mysterious or profound.
insensible: Imperceptible.
insinuate: To imply.

insipid: Tasteless.
insouciant: Nonchalant.
Instigate: urge, incite
insurrection: The state of being in active resistance to authority.
Intelligible: understandable, comprehensible
interdict: Authoritative act of prohibition.
interim: Time between acts or periods.
intransigent: Not capable of being swayed or diverted from a course.
Intransigent: stubborn, uncompromising
Intrepid: bold, fearless
intrepid: Fearless and bold.
Intrinsic: essential nature of a thing
introspection: The act of observing and analyzing one's own thoughts and feelings.
Intuitive: known through immediate insight not gained through rational thought
inundate: To fill with an overflowing abundance.
inure: To harden or toughen by use, exercise, or exposure.
invalid: One who is disabled by illness or injury.
invective: An utterance intended to cast censure, or reproach.
inveigh: To utter vehement censure or invective.

Inveigle: acquire through sneakiness
inveterate: Habitual.
invidious: Showing or feeling envy.
invincible: Not to be conquered, subdued, or overcome.
iota: A small or insignificant mark or part.
irascible: Prone to anger.
irate: Moved to anger.
ire: Wrath.
Iridescent: having shiny rainbow colors, shimmery
irksome: Wearisome.
Isolate: to separate and make alone or single
itinerant: Wandering.
itinerate: To wander from place to place.
Jargon: specialized vocabulary
Jeer: taunt, deride
jocular: Inclined to joke.
jovial: Merry.
judicious: Prudent.
Juggernaut: large vehicle that crushes anything in its path
junta: A council or assembly that deliberates in secret upon the affairs of government.

Labile: unstable, open to change
Labyrinth: maze
lachrymose: Given to shedding tears.
lackadaisical: Listless.
Laconic: few words, reticent
Lactate: to produce milk
languid: Relaxed.
lascivious: Lustful.
lassitude: Lack of vitality or energy.
latent: Dormant.
Latent: potential, hidden quality
Lateral: sideways, on the side
laudable: Praiseworthy.
laudatory: Pertaining to, expressing, or containing praise.
legacy: A bequest.
levee: An embankment beside a river or stream or an arm of the sea, to prevent overflow.
levity: Frivolity.
Levity: lightness, good humor
lexicon: A dictionary.
libel: Defamation.
licentious: Wanton.

lien: A legal claim or hold on property, as security for a debt or charge.
Limpid: clear, serene, transparent`
Lionize: make much of
listless: Inattentive.
lithe: Supple.
Loquacioius: extremely talkative and articulate
loquacious: Talkative.
Lucid: clear, understandable
Ludicrous: ridiculous, absurd
lugubrious: Indicating sorrow, often ridiculously.
luminary: One of the heavenly bodies as a source of light.
lustrous: Shining.
malaise: A condition of uneasiness or ill-being.
malcontent: One who is dissatisfied with the existing state of affairs.
malevolence: Ill will.
Malevolent: evil, having evil intent
malign: To speak evil of, especially to do so falsely and severely.
malleable: Pliant.
massacre: The unnecessary and indiscriminate killing of human beings.

maudlin: Foolishly and tearfully affectionate.
Maverick: intrepid person, innovator
mawkish: Sickening or insipid.
mellifluous: Sweetly or smoothly flowing.
mendacious: Untrue.
mendicant: A beggar.
meretricious: Alluring by false or gaudy show.
mesmerize: To hypnotize.
Meticulous: extremely careful, fastidious
meticulous: Over-cautious.
mettle: Courage.
mettlesome: Having courage or spirit.
microcosm: The world or universe on a small scale.
mien: The external appearance or manner of a person.
Misanthrope: one who hates humanity
mischievous: Fond of tricks.
miscreant: A villain.
miser: A person given to saving and hoarding unduly.
misnomer: A name wrongly or mistakenly applied.
moderation: Temperance.

modicum: A small or token amount.
mollify: To soothe.
molt: To cast off, as hair, feathers, etc.
Monolith: a single, huge structure, or a large organization acting as one force
monomania: The unreasonable pursuit of one idea.
morbid: Caused by or denoting a diseased or unsound condition of body or mind.
mordant: Biting.
moribund: On the point of dying.
morose: Gloomy.
Mosaic: picture made of many small parts such as tiles
Multifarious: diverse, of great variety
multifarious: Having great diversity or variety.
Mundane: everything, pedestrain
mundane: Worldly, as opposed to spiritual or celestial.
munificent: Extraordinarily generous.
myriad: A vast indefinite number.
Nadir: low point, point opposite the zenith
nadir: The lowest point.
Naivete: unsophisticatedness, artlessness

nefarious: Wicked in the extreme.
negligent: Apt to omit what ought to be done.
Negligible: insignificant, not to be considered
neophyte: Having the character of a beginner.
Nexus: connection, center
noisome: Very offensive, particularly to the sense of smell.
nostrum: Any scheme or recipe of a charlatan character.
noxious: Hurtful.
Nuance: slight distinction
Nucleate: to cluster, to form a nucleus
nugatory: Having no power or force.
Nugatory: negligible, having no effect
Nullify: negate, make invalid
obdurate: Impassive to feelings of humanity or pity.
Obdurate: stubborn, unfeeling
obfuscate: To darken; to obscure.
Objective: empirically provable, existing independently
oblique: Slanting; said of lines.
Oblivious: unknowing, unheeding

Obscure: to hide or hidden, vague, not easily understood
obsequious: Showing a servile readiness to fall in with the wishes or will of another.
Obsequious: sycophantic-flatter, fawning
Obstinate: stubborn, unmoving
obstreperous: Boisterous.
obtrude: To be pushed or to push oneself into undue prominence.
obtrusive: Tending to be pushed or to push oneself into undue prominence.
Obtuse: difficult to understand, unable to understand, stupid
obviate: To clear away or provide for, as an objection or difficulty.
Occlude: to obstruct, block up
odious: Hateful.
odium: A feeling of extreme repugnance, or of dislike and disgust.
officious: Intermeddling with what is not one's concern.
ominous: Portentous.
onerous: Burdensome or oppressive.
onus: A burden or responsibility.
Opaque: not transparent, not letting light through

opprobrium: The state of being scornfully reproached or accused of evil.
Orate: to make a speech, esp. pompously
Orthodox: adhering to a strict set of beliefs
ossify: To convert into bone.
Ostensible: apparent, under pretext
ostentation: A display dictated by vanity and intended to invite applause or flattery.
ostracism: Exclusion from intercourse or favor, as in society or politics.
ostracize: To exclude from public or private favor.
palate: The roof of the mouth.
palatial: Magnificent.
palliate: To cause to appear less guilty.
palpable: Perceptible by feeling or touch.
panacea: A remedy or medicine proposed for or professing to cure all diseases.
Pandemonium: noisy chaos, bedlam
panegyric: A formal and elaborate eulogy, written or spoken, of a person or of an act.
panoply: A full set of armor.
Paradigm: model, theoretical framework
Paradox: seeming contradiction or an actual contradiction
paragon: A model of excellence.

Paragon: an ideal, perfect model
Pariah: A member of a degraded class; a social outcast.
paroxysm: A sudden outburst of any kind of activity.
Parry: fend off, dodge
parsimonious: Unduly sparing in the use or expenditure of money.
partisan: Characterized by or exhibiting undue or unreasoning devotion to a party.
pathos: The quality in any form of representation that rouses emotion or sympathy.
paucity: Fewness.
peccadillo: A small breach of propriety or principle.
Pedantic: overly scholarly
pedestrian: One who journeys on foot.
Peer: equal
pellucid: Translucent.
penchant: A bias in favor of something.
penurious: Excessively sparing in the use of money.
penury: Indigence.
peregrination: A wandering.
peremptory: Precluding question or appeal.

perfidy: Treachery.
perfunctory: Half-hearted.
peripatetic: Walking about.
Peripheral: outside, surrounding, auxiliary
perjury: A solemn assertion of a falsity.
permeate: To pervade.
pernicious: Tending to kill or hurt.
persiflage: Banter.
Perspicacious: keen, mentally sharp
perspicacity: Acuteness or discernment.
Pertinent: clearly relevant
Perturb: to disquiet, upset
perturbation: Mental excitement or confusion.
Peruse: study thoroughly
Pervasive: throughout, in every part
petrify: To convert into a substance of stony hardness and character.
petulant: Displaying impatience.
Phenomenon: an occurrence
phlegmatic: Not easily roused to feeling or action.
physiognomy: The external appearance merely.
Pied: multi- colored and blotchy

Pigment: coloring element in paint
pious: Religious.
Piquant: spicy, as in hot sauce, stimulating, provocative
Pique: offense, resentment, provoke or excite
pique: To excite a slight degree of anger in.
Placate: please, pacify
placate: To bring from a state of angry or hostile feeling to one of patience or friendliness.
Placid: quiet, calm
Plasticity: malleability, stretchiness
Platitude: a trite saying, bromide
platitude: A written or spoken statement that is flat, dull, or commonplace.
plea: An argument to obtain some desired action.
plenary: Entire.
plethora: Excess; superabundance.
Plethora: multiplicity, excessive amount
plumb: A weight suspended by a line to test the verticality of something.
plummet: A piece of lead for making soundings, adjusting walls to the vertical.
Plummet: to fall suddenly
poignant: Severely painful or acute to the spirit.

polyglot: Speaking several tongues.
ponderous: Unusually weighty or forcible.
Pontifical: like a pontiff, pope, extremely authoritative
Porous: having pores, having minute holes
portend: To indicate as being about to happen, especially by previous signs.
portent: Anything that indicates what is to happen.
Prate: chatter, talk meaninglessly
Prattle: babble, as a child
precarious: Perilous.
Precedent: earlier example setting a rule
Precipitate: sudden or steep, rain, snow, to bring about suddenly
preclude: To prevent.
precocious: Having the mental faculties prematurely developed.
Precursor: a necessary predecessor
Predestine: determined ahead of time
predominate: To be chief in importance, quantity, or degree.
premature: Coming too soon.
presage: To foretell.
Prescience: ability to foretell events

prescience: Knowledge of events before they take place.
presumption: That which may be logically assumed to be true until disproved.
preternatural: Extraordinary.
Prevalent: common, frequent
prevalent: Of wide extent or frequent occurrence.
Prevaricate: lie
prevaricate: To use ambiguous or evasive language for the purpose of deceiving or diverting attention.
prim: Stiffly proper.
pristine: Primitive.
Probity: honesty
probity: Virtue or integrity tested and confirmed.
proclivity: A natural inclination.
Proclivity: tendency
procrastination: Delay.
Proctor: one who supervises students at an exam
Prodigal: foolishly generous, not thrifty
prodigal: One wasteful or extravagant, especially in the use of money or property.
prodigious: Immense.
Prodigy: very talented child

profligacy: Shameless viciousness.
Profligate: extravagent, prodigal
profligate: Recklessly wasteful
Profound: deep, thoughtful
Profuse: plentiful
profuse: Produced or displayed in overabundance.
Proliferate: multiply, procreate
prolix: Verbose.
Prologue: introductory passage
Prone: inclined, or the position of lying face down
Propensity: inclination
propinquity: Nearness.
propitious: Kindly disposed.
Propriety: appropriateness, social acceptability
prosaic: Unimaginative.
Proscribe: condemn, forbid
proscribe: To reject, as a teaching or a practice, with condemnation or denunciation.
protuberant: Bulging.
provident: Anticipating and making ready for future wants or emergencies.
Provocative: tending to simulate

prudence: Caution.
puerile: Childish.
pugnacious: Quarrelsome.
Pulverize: smash into dust
punctilious: Strictly observant of the rules or forms prescribed by law or custom.
pungency: The quality of affecting the sense of smell.
Pungent: strong tasting or smelling
pusillanimous: Without spirit or bravery.
pyre: A heap of combustibles arranged for burning a dead body.
qualm: A fit of nausea.
quandary: A puzzling predicament.
Querulous: complaining, whining
quibble: An utterly trivial distinction or objection.
quiescence: Being quiet, still, or at rest; inactive
quiescent: Being in a state of repose or inaction.
Quisling: traitor
Quixotic: Chivalrous or romantic to a ridiculous or extravagant degree.
Quorum: number of members of a governing body necessary in order to proceed
quotidian: Of an everyday character; ordinary.

raconteur: A person skilled in telling stories.
ramify: To divide or subdivide into branches or subdivisions.
rapacious: Seize by force, avaricious
raucous: Harsh.
reactionary: Pertaining to, of the nature of, causing, or favoring reaction.
rebuff: A peremptory or unexpected rejection of advances or approaches.
recalcitrant: Marked by stubborn resistance.
Recalcitrant: stubborn, defiant
recant: To withdraw formally one's belief (in something previously believed or maintained).
Recapitulate: to repeat, sum up
Reciprocate: to give and take, to return, to pay back
reciprocity: Equal mutual rights and benefits granted and enjoyed.
recluse: One who lives in retirement or seclusion.
recondite: Incomprehensible to one of ordinary understanding.
Reconnaissance: survey, esp military action
recrudescent: Becoming raw or sore again.
Recumbent: lying down, resting
recuperate: To recover.

Redolent: aromatic, having an odor
Redoubtable: formidable, illustrious
redoubtable: Formidable.
redress: To set right, as a wrong by compensation or the punishment of the wrong-doer.
Redundant: repetitive, and thus unnecessary
refractory: Not amenable to control.
Refute: to disprove, to argue against
regale: To give unusual pleasure.
regicide: The killing of a king or sovereign.
reiterate: To say or do again and again.
relapse: To suffer a return of a disease after partial recovery.
Relic: remnant, souvenir, venerated object
Relinquish: to let go of, give up
remonstrate: To present a verbal or written protest to those who have power to right or prevent a wrong.
Renegade: an outlaw, one who is unconventional
renovate: To restore after deterioration, as a building.
repast: A meal; figuratively, any refreshment.
repel: To force or keep back in a manner, physically or mentally.
repine: To indulge in fretfulness and faultfinding.

Reprobate: depraved, condemned
reprobate: One abandoned to depravity and sin.
repudiate: To refuse to have anything to do with.
repulsive: Grossly offensive.
requisite: Necessary.
requite: To repay either good or evil to, as to a person.
rescind: To make void, as an act, by the enacting authority or a superior authority.
resilience: The power of springing back to a former position
Resolute: determined, faithful
resonance: Able to reinforce sound by sympathetic vibrations.
respite: Interval of rest.
restive: Resisting control.
Resuscitate: to revive, renew
Reticent: not talkative
retinue: The group of people who accompany an important person during travels.
Retract: take back, recant
revere: To regard with worshipful veneration.
reverent: Humble.
ribald: Indulging in or manifesting coarse indecency or obscenity.

Rift: a gap or fissure
risible: Capable of exciting laughter.
Riveting: commanding full attention, fascinating
rotund: Round from fullness or plumpness.
Rudimentary: basic
ruffian: A lawless or recklessly brutal fellow.
ruminate: To chew over again, as food previously swallowed and regurgitated.
Runic: like runes, mysterious, secret
sagacious: Able to discern and distinguish with wise perception.
salacious: Having strong sexual desires.
Salient: noticeable, prominent
salient: Standing out prominently.
salubrious: Healthful; promoting health.
salutary: Beneficial.
sanction: To approve authoritatively.
sanguine: Cheerfully confident; optimistic.
sardonic: Scornfully or bitterly sarcastic.
satiate: To satisfy fully the appetite or desire of.
satyr: A very lascivious person.
Saunter: to walk in an easygoing swagger
savor: To perceive by taste or smell.

scabbard: The sheath of a sword or similar bladed weapon.
scintilla: The faintest ray.
scribble: Hasty, careless writing.
Scruple: have moral qualms about, moral principle
Secrete: give off or to hide
sedulous: Persevering in effort or endeavor.
Seine: fishnet
Seminal: original or relating to seed or semen
sequence: The order in which a number or persons, things, or events follow one another in space or time.
sequential:in order, arranged serially
Sever: to cut off completely
severance: Separation.
shard:fragment esp glass or pottery
Shirk: neglect or ignore
shrewd: Characterized by skill at understanding and profiting by circumstances.
Simulate: imitate, make seem real
sinecure: Any position having emoluments with few or no duties.
sinuous: Curving in and out.
skiff: Usually, a small light boat propelled by oars.

sluggard: A person habitually lazy or idle.
solace: Comfort in grief, trouble, or calamity.
Solicitude: over-attentive care, anxiety
solvent: Having sufficient funds to pay all debts.
somniferous: Tending to produce sleep.
somnolent: Sleepy.
sonorous: Resonant.
sophistry: Reasoning sound in appearance only, especially when designedly deceptive.
soporific: Causing sleep; also, something that causes sleep.
sordid: Filthy, morally degraded
Specious: having the deceptive look of truth
specious: Plausible.
Spectrum: range of all colors, complete range
Sporadic: occasional, infrequent
Spurious: false, fradulent
spurious: Not genuine.
squalid: Having a dirty, mean, poverty-stricken appearance.
squalid: Having a dirty, mean, poverty-stricken appearance.
Stagnant: stale, foul, motionless
stanch: To stop the flowing of; to check.

stanch: To stop the flowing of; to check.

Stasis: stagnation, equilibrium

Stereotype: generalized judgment of a group

stigma: A mark of infamy or token of disgrace attaching to a person as the result of evil-doing.

stigma: A mark of infamy or token of disgrace attaching to a person as the result of evil-doing.

stingy: Cheap, unwilling to spend money.

Stipple: speckle or fleck esp with paint, effect of many small dots

stolid: Expressing no power of feeling or perceiving.

Strata: layer

Striate: to stripe

Subjective: relating to the mind as the subject of experience

submerge: To place or plunge under water.

Subordinate: depending on, subservient

subterfuge: Evasion.

Succinct: concise, stating in few words

succinct: Concise.

sumptuous: Rich and costly.

supercilious: Exhibiting haughty and careless contempt.

Superfluity: excess

superfluous: Being more than is needed.
Superfluous: excess, extra
supernumerary: Superfluous.
supersede: To displace.
Supersede: to supplant
supine: Lying on the back.
supplicate: To beg.
Suppress: keep secret, contain, inhibit
suppress: To prevent from being disclosed or punished.
surcharge: An additional amount charged.
surfeit: To feed to fullness or to satiety.
susceptibility: A specific capability of feeling or emotion.
Susceptible: prone to, open to
sybarite: A luxurious person.
Sybil: witch
sycophant: A servile flatterer, especially of those in authority or influence.
Synchronous: at the same time
synopsis: A syllabus or summary.
Synthesis: the combination of diverse elements into one
Tacit: unspoken yet understood

taciturn: Disinclined to conversation.
Tangential: peripheral, no on the subject at hand
Tantalize: tease, give taste of
Tapestry: decorative wall hanging
taut: Stretched tight.
temerity: Foolhardy disregard of danger; recklessness.
Temperament: disposition, sensibility
Tentative: hesitant, uncertain
Tenuous: not solid, weak
Tepid: lukewarm, room temperature
terse: Pithy.
Terse: short, curt
timorous: Lacking courage.
Timorous: timid, fearful
Tirade: long, harsh, highly critical speech
torpid: Dull; sluggish; inactive.
Torque: rotational force, twist
torrid: Excessively hot.
tortuous: Abounding in irregular bends or turns.
Tortuous: twisting, winding, tricky
Tout: solicit or promote

tractable: Easily led or controlled.
Transcendental: abstract, supernatural
transgress: To break a law.
transient: One who or that which is only of temporary existence.
transitory: Existing for a short time only.
Transpose: change from one place to mode to another
travail: Hard or agonizing labor.
travesty: A grotesque imitation.
Travesty: mockery, parody
trenchant: Cutting deeply and quickly.
trepidation: Nervous uncertainty of feeling.
trite: Made commonplace by frequent repetition.
Trivial: minor, not important
Troupe: group of performers
truculence: Ferocity.
Truculent: ferocious, extremely harsh
truculent: Having the character or the spirit of a savage.
turbid: In a state of turmoil; muddled
Turbid: muddy, obscured
turgid: Swollen.

turpitude: Depravity.
tutelage: The act of training or the state of being under instruction.
tyro: One slightly skilled in or acquainted with any trade or profession.
ubiquitous: Being present everywhere.
Ubiquitous: everywhere, in all places
ulterior: Not so pertinent as something else to the matter spoken of.
umbrage: A sense of injury.
Unassailable: not questionable, not doubtable
unctuous: Oily.
undermine: To subvert in an underhand way.
undulate: To move like a wave or in waves.
Unprepossessing: homely, plain
untoward: Causing annoyance or hindrance.
upbraid: To reproach as deserving blame.
Urbane: sophisticated, wordly
vagary: A sudden desire or action
vainglory: Excessive, pretentious, and demonstrative vanity.
valorous: Courageous.
vapid: Having lost sparkling quality and flavor.
Vapid: uninteresting, without liveliness

Variance: difference, disagreement
variegated: Having marks or patches of different colors; also, varied.
vehement: Very eager or urgent.
venal: Mercenary, corrupt.
veneer: Outside show or elegance.
venial: That may be pardoned or forgiven, a forgivable sin.
veracious: Habitually disposed to speak the truth.
Veracity: truthfulness
veracity: Truthfulness.
Verbiage: excessive wordiness
verbiage: Use of many words without necessity.
verbose: Wordy.
verdant: Green with vegetation.
veritable: Real; true; genuine.
Vernacular: common speech, ordinary language
vestige: A visible trace, mark, or impression, of something absent, lost, or gone.
Vestige: remnant, trace
Viable: capable of living, capable of working
vicissitude: A change, especially a complete change of condition or circumstances, as of fortune.

vigilance: Alert and intent mental watchfulness in guarding against danger.
vigilant: Being on the alert to discover and ward off danger or insure safety.
Vindictive: vengeful, spiteful
virago: Loud talkative women, strong statured women
virtu: Rare, curious, or beautiful quality.
visage: The face, countenance, or look of a person.
Viscous: having a thick consistency, gelatinous
vitiate: To contaminate.
Vituperate: scold with excessively harsh language
vituperate: To overwhelm with wordy abuse.
vivify: To endue with life.
vociferous: Making a loud outcry.
volatile: Changeable.
Volatile: unstable, likely to explode or vaporize
Voluble: fluent, talkative
voluble: Having great fluency in speaking.
wean: To transfer (the young) from dependence on mother's milk to another form of nourishment.
Welter: chaotic mess
whimsical: Capricious.

Whimsy: caprice, a playful thing
winsome: Attractive.
Zeal: fanatical enthusiasm
Zealot: one who has great enthusiasm esp for a cause
Zeitgeist: The intellectual and moral tendencies that characterize any age or epoch.

Preparation for the LSAT exam could be very tedious, but it's a rewarding experience.
The LSAT is well structured and organized as the test makers put in significant work to curb any gimmick that could affect its credibility.

For LSAT test preparation, there are no shortcuts, and you have to be smart to score high. You have to improve your reading and thinking skills over time. LSAT should not be viewed as a compulsory hurdle put in front of you as a prerequisite for law school. Instead, it should be seen as a learning process and an opportunity to improve on one's reasoning ability and decision-making process.
Aside from passing the LSAT, the skills acquired will also help one excel to become a successful attorney.
One of the essential skills required in law school is the ability to read. The reading material is so bulky, but you are expected to complete it efficiently. Also, for a student to be successful in law, he must attain mastery in persuasion and argumentation.

These tools are necessary for an attorney to excel in his/her career. And finally, every attorney needs to have a keen sense of logic; they must also understand the technical procedural rules which are all embedded in the LSAT prep.

As you prepare for LSAT, I want you to relax, prepare well, and have a bit of fun.
Give it your best shot because it will worth it in the end when you start receiving admission and scholarship offers from top law schools in the country and beyond. Those who attach minimal seriousness to the LSAT prep are not helping themselves. They limit their chances of gaining admission, and they also fail to enhance their skills, which will be needed to pass law school and the bar exam.

10 Fantastic LSAT Prep Tips

LSAT Tip #1: Take the LSAT Early
The best time to take the LSAT is in February or June of the year prior to when you plan to enter law school. Many law schools accept applications beginning in early December and ending in February or March, and make admissions decisions on a rolling basis. Law schools will receive February and June LSAT scores early in the admission process, increasing your changes of being accepted.
LSAT Tip #2: Prepare Early
It is best to start test preparation 8-12 weeks prior to the test date. This is not a college exam, so you cannot "cram" for it in the last couple of week or

days. The preparation regimen should include mastering the various question types and getting accustomed to the rigor of taking the LSAT exam. This takes time.

LSAT Tip #3: Take Full Length Practice Tests

Throughout your preparation period, take practice tests 1-3 times a week. Simulate actual test conditions as much as possible. Doing so will help your mind and body build up the necessary stamina to make it through the entire LSAT test without losing energy and focus.

LSAT Tip #4: Learn from Your Mistakes

Your 8-12 weeks of LSAT prep time should involve completing hundreds of practice questions. But just doing questions will provide only marginal help in achieving the best LSAT score you are capable of achieving. After completing practice questions you must review the answers to figure out where your reasoning was correct or incorrect. Learn from your errors so that you are less likely to repeat them. This is the way to master the LSAT.

LSAT Tip #5: Enroll in an LSAT Prep Class

The advantage of taking an LSAT prep class such as the LSAT Princeton Review or the Kaplan LSAT test prep course is that the class will help jump start your study regimen and help you understand how to do well on the LSAT. The instructors will help you understand each question type and be available to answer questions. Also, you will receive hundreds of practice questions and have access to every released past LSAT.

LSAT Tip #6: Get Extra Prep Assistance

If you find that despite your best efforts you are not making the progress that you expect in LSAT prep, get additional help. Find a tutor that will give you

LSAT advice and one-on-one attention to guide you through your difficult period.

LSAT Tip #7: Avoid Burnout

Although some level of anxiety is likely unavoidable, it is important to minimize it. Pace yourself and resist the urge to study too much as doing so may cause you to become mentally drained. Incorporate into your LSAT study schedule activities that will help reduce your stress, such as going to the gym.

LSAT Tip #9: Answer Each Question

Do not skip any question. Even if you have no clue as to the correct answer, guessing will not harm you, but might help you. An LSAT score is based on correct answers, without penalty for incorrect or blank answers. However, if you leave a question blank you have a 0% chance of earning a point for that question. If you guess at a multiple choice question where there are 5 possible answers, you have a 20% chance of earning a point for that question.

LSAT Tip #9: Do not Obsess After the LSAT

Keep in mind that after the LSAT there is nothing you can do about your performance. There is no reason to obsess about questions you think you got wrong, or to go into a panic, believing that your score will be low. Instead, spend at least a few moments basking in the relief that it is over. Then focus on other items on your law school admissions checklist such as completing law school applications!

If you do not perform as well on the LSAT as you wanted to, do not panic. You can retake the test. However, before making that decision you have to consider whether it is likely that your score will improve significantly, as statistics show that in the absence of a specific, identifiable factor that caused the poor performance, retaking the LSAT will only improve a score by 2.5 points. Also, while your score may be lower than you would have liked, it might be good enough for the law schools to which you plan to apply. So instead of panicking, calmly figure out what your next step should be.

Stress and Time Management

There is no single perfect way to achieve LR success. Try multiple methods and identify what works for you. A successful approach will get you the correct answer quickly and will simplify the process. Your approach needs to work in approximately 1 minute and 25 seconds per question (the exact time per question varies by the number of questions per test: 24 or 26). Lawyering is a high-stress profession; you have to think quickly on your feet. That the LSAT emphasizes speed and psychology-under-pressure isn't a bug; it's a feature.

Ladder of Difficulty

LSAT questions tend to become more difficult as the section progresses. This means that low scoring students should focus on the earlier questions as they will tend to be easier. If you aren't a good LSAT student, skipping the final few questions altogether might be a good idea. Those harder questions at the end count as much as the easier ones at the beginning.

Diet tips for maintaining top mental health

These days nearly everyone recognizes that the foods they eat affect the appearance of their bodies, however most people fail to realize that what they consume also has a considerable impact on how their brains work. Your diet can affect your brain's energy level, memory, and the efficiency with which it handles its tasks.

The brain is an exceptionally active metabolic organ, which means that it must constantly consume energy to function. Still, the brain is a picky eater. Research has consistently shown that foods with the right neurochemicals – which will be outlined shortly – can help you concentrate, tune sensorimotor skills, stay motivated, magnify memory, increase reaction times, defuse stress, and, to a certain extent, even prevent mental aging.

Fats

While a healthy brain is determined in part by how much (or little) fat you eat, the more important factor is the kind of fat consumed. Maximum intellectual performance requires a specific type of fat known as omega-3 fatty acids, found most commonly in fish. So to ensure that your diet is rich in omega-3 fats, and that your brain is flush with this powerful nutrient, it is recommended that you eat plenty of oily fish like salmon, sardines, trout, tuna, herring, mackerel, and anchovies.

Proteins

Eating protein raises the levels of an amino acid called tyrosine, which prompts the brain to manufacture norepinephrine and dopamine, important chemical messengers in the brain. Norepinephrine and dopamine serve to keep you energized as they stimulate receptors in the brain specific to alertness and activity. Poultry, seafood, soy products, and lean meat are the richest sources of protein, and dairy products, legumes, nuts, and seeds contain high concentrations as well.

Carbohydrates

Glucose from carbohydrates provides the fuel your brain uses to produce energy. Be careful, however, when choosing your sources of carbohydrates! The key is to choose carbohydrates that are broken down by the body gradually and provide a steady, long-term source of energy (typically known as complex carbohydrates), as opposed to carbohydrates that have an immediate impact on the body and cause a rapid burst of energy that will fade quickly (simple carbohydrates). Whole grain foods such as cereals, wheat bran, and whole wheat pasta are key sources of complex carbohydrates. Fruits and vegetables are another excellent source of carbohydrates that can provide long-lasting energy. Refined sugars are the most common simple carbohydrates and, as mentioned previously, only fuel the brain for a short period of time and ultimately result in a demanding drop of energy or "crash." Avoid refined sugars whenever possible.

Vitamins and Minerals

In addition to the foods discussed above, it is also a good idea to consider supplementing your diet with specific vitamins and minerals designed to promote proper body function. The 'B' complex vitamins are particularly important as they play a vital role in producing energy. Vitamins A, C, and E are powerful antioxidants and promote and preserve memory. Good sources of these vitamins include blueberries and other berries, red grapes, tomatoes, broccoli, garlic, spinach, carrots, whole grains, and soy.

Minerals are also critical to mental functioning and performance. Magnesium and manganese are crucial for sustained brain energy. Sodium, potassium, and calcium are also important in the thinking process as they facilitate the transmission of neurochemical messages in the brain. An easy way to get most of your important vitamins and minerals is to simply take a multivitamin each day.

The final key component in maintaining a healthy and efficient brain is also the most simplest and most readily available: water. Studies have shown that the vast majority of adults do not consume enough water daily and the consequences can be severe. Even mildly dehydration decreases your mental energy significantly, impairing memory and cognitive function. In fact, as little as a 2% drop in body water can cause faulty short-term memory, trouble with basic math, and difficulty focusing on a computer screen or on a printed page for more than a few seconds at a time. To stay properly hydrated, try to drink at least three liters of water per day.

With all of this in mind, here are a few night-before-the test dinners, and before-the-test breakfast suggestions:

Dinner the night before the test

– omega-3 fatty fish (or lean meat) with spinach or broccoli, and potatoes or a few pieces of whole grain bread. Remember to drink plenty of water!

Try to have your dinner at least two to three hours before you go to bed to ensure a good night's sleep without an overly full stomach.

Breakfast the morning of the test

– eggs, oatmeal (or whole grain cereal, or a piece of wheat toast with peanut butter), and fresh fruit or juice.

Also, beware of coffee or other caffeinated drinks before the test as they tend to have the same detrimental effects as sugar, with unpredictable boosts of energy/jitters followed by crashes and fatigue.

Avoid potential disaster by eating for your brain for at least a few days leading up to the test so you're sure that you won't have any unpleasant reactions to foods that you may not normally consume.

Should You Take an LSAT Prep Course?

LSAT prep courses are expensive, especially when you compare their cost to purchasing other study materials online. Studies show, however, that students who take a live study course perform 2-5 points better than students who don't. If at all possible, take a preparation course, as they can be very meaningful to your LSAT score. Even if you only get a two-point bump in your score, this investment is well worth the money and effort.

Many people will tell you can do a self-study as a prep course if you have enough discipline. You will often hear "If you are the type that needs structure to stay focused, or need a confidence boost, you should take the class. If not, don't worry about it."

Despite this advice, here is why every serious student should take a live prep course:

1. 2-5 points could save you $50,000 to $100,000 in law school tuition. Law schools offer scholarships to the strongest candidates.

2. While the average advantage is 2-5 points, your improvement could be much larger. There are plenty of examples of people who have improved 10 or more points after attending these courses.

3. Paying for the course will reinforce your discipline.

4. Live instructors can specifically identify your individual weaknesses and can give you good feedback. Often instructors will alert you to weaknesses that you didn't know you had. A live course also gives you a resource for accurate, timely answers to your questions.

5. Courses cover everything you need to know, forcing you to learn things you otherwise might have skipped or ignored.

6. Courses conduct several formal, timed LSATs. You will get a real test experience to gauge how you are doing.

So while many of us think we have the self-discipline to achieve these results without spending the money, why would you want to risk it when this is truly your future on the line? Unless it is simply not a financial option for you to take a live course, the benefits are substantial enough for you to not hesitate in taking a live course.

Top Ranked LSAT Prep Courses

ALPHA SCORE LSAT PREP

Compact, Engaging Course: Alpha Score's straightforward and engaging lectures make studying for the LSAT quick and even enjoyable. Videos, animations and explanations help you learn to think like the test makers, so you'll know why certain answers are right or wrong. Alpha Score's course provides the essential tools and strategies to solve even the most difficult problems one step at a time.

Personalized Help From Instructors: There are no live course options, but you can get one-on-one help if you crave a more interactive study experience than the HD video lectures. Seasoned LSAT instructors are available to help you navigate your weaker areas and provide customized homework and additional guidance if you need it.

Price: It's always nice to find a very effective course at that is also a bargain. Alpha Score offers a range of study materials at an excellent price. At several hundred dollars less than the competition, it's worth it to use Alpha Score to supplement another LSAT review course you've already purchased, although it's a comprehensive course all by itself!

Video Playback Speed: You can speed up or slow down a video lecture to save time or to give yourself more time to absorb the information. Listen to the lecture at 1.5x or 2x the original speed, or slow it down to take notes. A self-paced course should move at the speed you determine – and Alpha Score helps make it happen.

LSATMAX PREP COURSES

Mobile App with Online Access: The LSATMax app is free to download and it comes with a ton of free content. You can watch the whiteboard video lessons, do daily drills, or complete Logic Games from anywhere. Best of all is the fact that LSATMax is the only company to offer users the ability to test the brand-new digital LSAT through their app's tablet-LSAT practice mode!

Price: Compared to some of its competitors, LSATMax's courses are pretty affordable; there's a nice range of packages to fit any budget. The app is free, with limited content, and you can customize your course based on how much practice you need. Lifetime access courses range from $749.99 for the Pro course to $949.99 for the Premium edition, while the Pro monthly subscription is $199/month. There's also 0% financing available for monthly payments.

Analytic Feedback: The LSATMax app calculates your overall performance in each section to pinpoint your strengths and weaknesses. This allows you to customize your study plan and concentrate on problem areas. Practice questions can also be filtered by type so you can focus on those areas that need the most practice.

Higher Score Guarantee: LSATMax offers a refund if you do not improve your LSAT score after completing the LSATMax course. Given the limited amount of time you can take the LSAT within a two year period, this makes spending your money on LSATMax much easier.

KAPLAN LSAT

Personalized Study: Kaplan provides customized recommendations for each student when it comes to preparing for the LSAT. Students are able to track their progress and identify areas that need improvement throughout the course so they can focus on those questions that will have the greatest impact on their score.

Higher Score Guarantee: If you have already taken the LSAT and do not improve your score you are eligible for a full refund from Kaplan. However, this guarantee only applies to their Advantage-Anywhere course option, not their On-Demand course.

No Free Demo: Kaplan does not offer free content or a mobile app to allow students to explore the course before they purchase. However, they do offer the option to take a free 90-minute preview class and a free practice test on their website.

MAGOOSH PREP LSAT

Price: In terms of value, you're not going to find a cheaper option that still delivers than the Magoosh LSAT prep. Even though it has a relatively low price, it still offers a plethora of helpful and unique features for test takers. You're not skimping on review materials just because you're paying a little less for this course.

Strategy: A great test-taking strategy is sometimes the last thing that students think of during preparation. Magoosh does the thinking for you in this regard, as its experts walk you through the best approaches for studying, provide helpful and constantly updated hints via the blog, and keep you focused on the main topic areas.

Simplicity: Sure, you're not going to get all of the fancy features that some of the more pricey courses come replete with, but that may be a benefit for some test takers. The Magoosh course is simple – it gives you the tools with which you need to succeed without overloading you with flashy dashboards or unnecessary graphics.

THE PRINCETON REVIEW LSAT

Personalized Instruction: Students can choose from a number of course options that give them access to one-on-one time with instructors if they need additional help with concepts or difficult questions. The small-group course and access to instructors outside of regularly scheduled sessions make The Princeton Review a popular option with students.

Quality and Quantity of Study Material: There are many course options to choose from, but all of them give students access to a broad range of practice questions, online drills and study material, proctored practice exams, and recorded video lessons. The Princeton Review stands by the quality of its instruction by offering generous satisfaction and money back guarantees as well.

No Mobile App: Courses emphasize the in-person and live online options and are not geared to portability beyond regular access to online materials from devices connected to the internet. Many students like the convenience and flexibility of studying for a few minutes whenever they get the chance on their smartphone or tablet; unfortunately, The Princeton Review has not yet developed an app for its LSAT courses.

TESTMASTERS LSAT

Diagnostic Scoring: TestMasters LSAT course comes with exam diagnostics that help students identify the areas that need the most improvement in order to achieve a high LSAT score. This self-guided prep course helps students focus on the questions they miss and therefore should spend the most time studying.

Database for Flawed Reasoning: TestMasters teaches students how to recognize and avoid common reasoning pitfalls. The extensive database provides examples of the flawed reasoning past students have used on real LSAT questions so that you don't make the same mistakes.

Limited Access: The course is only available to students for 100 days prior to the specific LSAT administration date students choose. Although this might help some students focus their efforts during the weeks immediately prior to the exam, many students prefer more time and flexibility to study.

BEST IN-PERSON LSAT PREP COURSE

Free Course Tour: Blueprint offers a free tour of their training materials. Students can explore various features before they purchase the course. Signing up for the free tour also gives you access to the June 2007 LSAT with video explanations to the questions and detailed scoring metrics for every LSAT that has been released.

Engaging Videos: What really stands out about this course is the animated and entertaining video instruction. The engaging and humorous delivery and animations help keep you focused while you are studying. The videos are short enough for students to process what is taught, and make it easier to retain the information for a longer period of time.

Video Sync Issues: In our tests, the audio was not precisely in sync with the video in several tutorials and lessons. This may have been due to broadband speed or issues with connectivity, so your mileage may vary. The Free Course Tour should give you an idea of how the course features will work for you.

POWERSCORE LSAT

Question Sets: Practice question sets consist of actual LSAT questions that are geared to the different categories you'll see on the exam. Some question sets are organized by level of difficulty, so students will know where they stand when it comes to solving the more challenging questions on the test.

Proven Materials: PowerScore is known for its popular LSAT study guide series, which includes the Logic Games Bible and the LSAT Reading Comprehension Bible. Although these books are not included in the course, the same techniques are used to help students master the material.

Low Quality Video: Much of the audio and video content has low quality. Although it is possible to understand the video lectures, the quality is lacking, particularly when compared to competitors.

7SAGE LSAT PREP

Price: 7Sage is one of the least expensive LSAT prep course options. For just $550 you can access their most comprehensive course, which includes 50 hours of video lessons and more than 4,000 problems that are explained in HD video.

No Tutoring Options: There is no option for additional help from trained staff or instructors. They do offer an extensive video library that has examples of how to solve many different LSAT practice problems, however, students who have questions about content that is not covered in the videos or need one-on-one help will need to look elsewhere.

BEST LSAT PREP COURSES – 2019 COMPARISON

LSAT Prep Courses	**Best For…**
LSATMax	Best Overall
Alpha Score	Engaging
Kaplan LSAT	Personalized Study
Princeton Review LSAT	Quality of Material

Magoosh LSAT	Most Affordable
Manhattan LSAT	Additional Tutoring

The Day of the Test

Have you been studying for the LSAT for months? Going to classes, reading textbooks, and trying out problems every day? Have you drilled all of your Logic Game types and figured out the secret to identifying every flaw known to humankind? That's awesome. But you're not done.

Sadly for us, there's a bit more to approaching the day of the LSAT than knowing all your material. As it turns out, the LSAC is extremely cautious (some might even say paranoid) about how people take the LSAT, so there are a *ton* of rules restricting what you can bring, wear, and do before and during the test.

Don't stress out, though! Just follow this checklist to make sure you're not going to break any rules and get kicked out on the day of the LSAT.

1. Don't forget your PRINTED admission ticket *and* a PRINTED photo.

Yes, seriously. The LSAC wants you to print out your admission ticket and bring it to the testing center.

Plus, they want you to print out a photo of yourself —but not just any old photo. It has to be *the same photo* that you uploaded to LSAC.org when making your LSAC account. If you bring a different photo, it's entirely plausible that you won't be allowed to take the test that day, so be careful!

Finally, although you should figure out where your testing center is way ahead of time, make sure to check your ticket *the night before* you take your test. Sometimes, testing centers can be changed last minute—and you don't want to assume that you'll be notified over email. Be prepared to print out a new ticket in case this happens.

(In fact, you may want to print spares of both your ticket and your photo!)

2. Also, don't forget your government-issued photo ID.

In addition to all that jazz, you'll also need a driver's license, passport, state ID, or similar government-issued photo identification on the day of the LSAT. The following forms of government issued ID are accepted:

- passport book
- passport card
- driver's license
- state or province-issued ID card
- US military ID card (Common Access Card, or CAC)—**NOT an acceptable form of ID for LSAT Writing**
- US Permanent Resident Card (Green Card)
- Canadian Permanent Resident Card
- national ID card
- consular ID card
- certain Canadian health care benefit cards

3. No Phone

The next bit of this list will be mostly electronic items, but this one's the toughest for students to grasp.
Don't bring your phone to the testing center.

Don't. Bring. Your. Phone. To. The. Testing. Center.

People *do* get kicked out—without a refund, with a black mark on their LSAT record—by simply bringing their phones on the day of the LSAT. It doesn't matter if it's on silent mode, or off, or stowed in your coat. You cannot have your phone.

Now, that's not to say that some kindly proctors won't ask to collect all the phones before the test starts, or be nice to you if you brought yours... But the theme of this day should be "Trust no one." Don't take a risk. Memorize or print out directions for getting to and from your test center (unless you can leave your phone in a car), and fight the urge to browse social media while you wait on test day.

One more time: don't bring your phone. There's an explicit zero-tolerance policy, so assume that if someone sees a phone on you at any point in the testing center, you'll be kicked out and will receive a score cancellation

4. No Mechanical Pencils
That's right—number 2 or HB wooden pencils only!

Why? Well, you wouldn't want to be the person stuck next to someone clicking their mechanical pencil over and over again for hours, would you? As a result, the LSAC prohibits mechanical pencils.

Make sure to bring enough pencils, erasers, and a non-electronic sharpener as well. You can't count on the testing center having any spares.

5. No Music Devices
No iPods. No Walkmans. No Zunes. (Writing that made me feel like a real grandpa.)

You're simply not allowed to have any music-playing devices, so that includes earbuds and headphones as well.

Seems like it's pretty easy to get bored after arriving to your testing center early and waiting for things to get going, right? Well, it's about to get worse...

6. No Stopwatch or Digital Watches

If you're not used to telling time on an analog watch, practice. That's the only way you can measure your timing on the LSAT, because digital watches and stopwatches are completely banned. (This includes fitness devices and other wearables as well, naturally.)

Why? Again, nobody wants to hear beeping going off during the test. Plus, the more electronics someone's allowed to take into the test, the easier it might be to cheat.

If you don't love analog watches, consider purchasing an LSAT watch. These measure 35-minute increments, perfect for the LSAT, and often color code different bits of time to show you how much you need to rush. Many of my students have bought these gizmos, although I can't personally attest to their use. (Just make sure to reset the watch for every section!)

You can't assume that your test room will have a visible clock, so do make sure you have *some* way of keeping time on the day of the LSAT.

7. No Hoodies, Hats or Sunglasses

Except for religious apparel and prescription eyeglasses, no headwear can be worn in the testing center. Even if it's a sunny day or you have terrible bedhead, ditch the shades and cap or risk losing your seat.

8. No Magazines, Books, Newspapers...etc....

No papers of any sort, in fact.

Sadly, this means you'll have little to distract you once you've checked in. If you find yourself getting bored, try meditating to calm your mind and center yourself—it'll pay dividends once you start the test.

9. Bring Snacks

Let's end on a sweet note: you're allowed to bring snacks and drinks to consume during your 15-minute break on the day of the LSAT!

That said, this wouldn't be the LSAT without some big restrictions on top of that. You can only bring snacks or drinks that will fit in a clear plastic ziplock bag of up to 1 gallon, which everything else you bring (wallet, keys, ID, medicine and hygiene products, pencils, eraser, highlighter, and so on) also has to fit into.

The beverages have to be either in a juice box or a plastic container, up to 20 ounces, and *can't* be in aluminum cans or glass containers. The snack can be pretty much whatever you want, although I'd recommend an assortment of fruits, nuts, and chocolate, so you keep your energy up and don't crash in section 5.

Law School Admissions Checklist

Junior Year

February (18 months before law school starts)

[ ] LSAT Prep – Plan on devoting at least 150 hours to this project. Either sign up for prep class or purchase Prep books and set up a self-study schedule.
[ ] Register with the Law School Admissions Council: http://www.lsac.org

March – May

[ ] Complete LSAT prep course or self study.

June

[ ] Sit for the LSAT
[ ] Determine the law schools that you will apply to

Senior Year

August (12 months before law school starts)

[ ] Find 2-3 professors who will agree to provide a letter of recommendation for you.
[ ] Provide each professor with a letter of recommendation preparation packet. Advise that you will follow up in 6 weeks.
[ ] Meet with undergraduate advisor to ensure that you are on track to graduate after the spring semester.
[ ] Begin writing your personal statement(s)

September

[ ] Update all materials (transcripts, etc…) with LSDAS.
[ ] Follow up with professors on any outstanding letters of recommendation. Be sure to have waited **6 weeks from request.**
[ ] Have a pre-law or faculty advisor review your completed personal statement(s)
[ ] Begin visiting prospective law schools (complete by October).

Mid-October – November 1.

[ ] Final proofreading of law school applications
[ ] Submit your law school applications

January – February (6 months before law school starts)
[ ] Update your Free Application for Federal Student Aid: http://www.fafsa.ed.gov
[ ] Supplement any outstanding law school applications if needed.
March - May
[ ] Make a final decision on which law school you will attend.
[ ] Notify any law school that has offered you a seat that you will decline as soon as you make the decision to decline.
[ ] Pay seat deposit to your law school.
[ ] Supplement your interest in any waitlist law schools.
[ ] Send your graduation transcript to your law school.

Conclusion

The LSAT is designed to evaluate skills that are vital for success in law school and ultimately for success as a practicing attorney. Reading comprehension questions test your ability to read, understand and analyze complex text. Logical reasoning questions require you to analyze and critically evaluate the reasoning and arguments of others. The analytical reasoning section evaluates your ability to take a set of facts and use deductive reasoning to make inferences. Furthermore, the LSAT tests your ability to accomplish all of these tasks quickly and efficiently. As you prepare for the LSAT it is important to be able to practice how to analyze and correctly answer each question type, but it is also important to practice doing so in the amount of time allotted. Therefore, timed practice tests are critical to your preparation and to receiving a good LSAT score.

Whether you take the February, June, October or December LSAT, the format is the same. The LSAT contains four scored sections, one unscored "experimental" section and an essay writing section. Each section is 35 minutes long. Of the scored sections, there are 2 Logical Reasoning sections with 24-26 questions each, giving you 1 minute and 20 seconds for each question. The Reading Comprehension section has 4 passages accompanied by five to seven questions per passage, for a total of 26-28 questions. The Analytical Reasoning (Logic Games) section has 4 "games," each accompanied by five to seven questions for each game, for a total of 23-24 questions. You have 8 minutes and 45 seconds to complete each of the 4 sections of the Reading Comprehension and 4 games of the Analytical Reasoning parts of the LSAT.

This does not mean, for example, that you must answer each Logical Reasoning question in exactly 1 minute, 20 seconds. Some questions will be easier for you to answer and will take less time. Other questions will take more time. The goal is that on average each question should take 1 minute, 20 seconds. If you end up spending 4 minutes on one tough LSAT Logical Reasoning question, you may find that you are unable to complete a few of the questions at the end of the test. Using a timer when you are answering practice questions will help you understand what it feels like to complete a question in approximately the right amount of time and what it feels like when you are on the verge of taking too much time. At that point you will know that it is time to "guess" and move on to the next question. Remember that on LSAT test day you will not be permitted to bring a timer into the LSAT test center. The only acceptable LSAT watch or time-keeping device that you can bring into the LSAT test locations is an analog watch. So practicing with a timer will help you get used to the time constraints even when you are not using a timer.

Another reason that a timer should be an integral part of your LSAT test preparation is that it is needed to simulate actual LSAT test conditions. Part of your preparation should be conditioning your mind and body so that they are able to handle the rigors of LSAT test day. Like any endurance activity, over time practice helps build stamina. Taking simulated LSATs throughout your preparation will help accomplish this. Use it to make sure that you take 35 minutes for each section and that you allow yourself only a 15 minute break after section 3. Also set your timer to give you a 5 minute warning before the end of each section, as the LSAT proctor will do on test day.

As you design your LSAT study schedule, it is important to plan to take 2-3 timed practice tests per week, along with completing daily practice questions. You will find as you progress through the 8-12 weeks of LSAT preparation that your score will steadily increase not only because you are getting fewer questions wrong on practice tests, but because you are completing more questions within the allotted time frame.

www.ingramcontent.com/pod-product-compliance
Lightning Source LLC
Chambersburg PA
CBHW061443031125
34901CB00012B/579
* 9 7 8 1 6 1 7 0 4 4 3 3 5 *